PROJECT MANAGEMENT BASICS

HOW TO MANAGE YOUR PROJECT WITH CHECKLISTS

Melanie McBride

Apress®

Project Management Basics: How to Manage Your Project with Checklists

Melanie McBride
Chandler, Arizona, USA

ISBN-13 (pbk): 978-1-4842-2085-6   ISBN-13 (electronic): 978-1-4842-2086-3
DOI 10.1007/978-1-4842-2086-3

Library of Congress Control Number: 2016949470

Managing Director: Welmoed Spahr
Acquisitions Editor: Robert Hutchinson
Development Editor: Matthew Moodie
Editorial Board: Steve Anglin, Pramila Balen, Laura Berendson, Aaron Black, Louise Corrigan, Jonathan Gennick, Robert Hutchinson, Celestin Suresh John, Nikhil Karkal, James Markham, Susan McDermott, Matthew Moodie, Natalie Pao, Gwenan Spearing
Coordinating Editor: Rita Fernando
Copy Editor: Brendan Frost
Compositor: SPi Global
Indexer: SPi Global
Cover Designer: Isaac Ruiz Soler

Distributed to the book trade worldwide by Springer Science+Business Media New York, 233 Spring Street, 6th Floor, New York, NY 10013. Phone 1-800-SPRINGER, fax (201) 348-4505, e-mail orders-ny@springer-sbm.com, or visit www.springeronline.com. Apress Media, LLC is a California LLC and the sole member (owner) is Springer Science + Business Media Finance Inc (SSBM Finance Inc). SSBM Finance Inc is a Delaware corporation.

For information on translations, please e-mail rights@apress.com, or visit www.apress.com.

Apress and friends of ED books may be purchased in bulk for academic, corporate, or promotional use. eBook versions and licenses are also available for most titles. For more information, reference our Special Bulk Sales–eBook Licensing web page at www.apress.com/bulk-sales.

Any source code or other supplementary materials referenced by the author in this text is available to readers at www.apress.com. For detailed information about how to locate your book's source code, go to www.apress.com/source-code/.

Printed on acid-free paper

Apress Business: The Unbiased Source of Business Information

Apress business books provide essential information and practical advice, each written for practitioners by recognized experts. Busy managers and professionals in all areas of the business world—and at all levels of technical sophistication—look to our books for the actionable ideas and tools they need to solve problems, update and enhance their professional skills, make their work lives easier, and capitalize on opportunity.

Whatever the topic on the business spectrum—entrepreneurship, finance, sales, marketing, management, regulation, information technology, among others—Apress has been praised for providing the objective information and unbiased advice you need to excel in your daily work life. Our authors have no axes to grind; they understand they have one job only—to deliver up-to-date, accurate information simply, concisely, and with deep insight that addresses the real needs of our readers.

It is increasingly hard to find information—whether in the news media, on the Internet, and now all too often in books—that is even-handed and has your best interests at heart. We therefore hope that you enjoy this book, which has been carefully crafted to meet our standards of quality and unbiased coverage.

We are always interested in your feedback or ideas for new titles. Perhaps you'd even like to write a book yourself. Whatever the case, reach out to us at editorial@apress.com and an editor will respond swiftly. Incidentally, at the back of this book, you will find a list of useful related titles. Please visit us at www.apress.com to sign up for newsletters and discounts on future purchases.

The Apress Business Team

For Paulette: "Plan the work; work the plan."

Contents

About the Author

 **Melanie McBride**, PMP, is a Technical Project Manager at Intel Corporation. With 20 years' experience managing projects in the semiconductor industry, she has worked variously as product development project manager, operations project manager, and vendor development manager. McBride is a recognized subject matter expert at Intel, where she writes a weekly blog on project management best practices. She speaks regularly at such professional conferences as PMI's Global Congress. She holds an MS in physics from Texas Tech University. McBride is the author of *Managing Projects in the Real World* (Apress, 2013).

Acknowledgments

If you're going to presume to write a "how-to" book about the basics of project management, then you must acknowledge the deep debt owed to the Project Management Institute for defining what those basics are in the first place. I'd especially like to thank the Phoenix, AZ chapter for the endless support from a community of like-minded people, especially Tom Stokes and the entire Chandler Breakfast Professional Development Meetings crew.

In large part, the idea for this book came to me through the mentoring I do, where I'm frequently asked for advice on how to get started in project management. These people are often intimidated by the magnitude of a project they need to manage, and I've found myself breaking down the basics for them over and over again. I'd like to extend a great big "thank you" to each of you who've approached me over the years. I hope that I helped you out!

For their longstanding support, I'd like to thank a few of the senior project managers I have the honor to know and work with. First, a big shout-out to Paulette Moore, who is never too busy to listen while I work out the right wording or strategy to tackle a difficult challenge. When Marc Conkle told me that he'd reluctantly loaned out his highlighted and dog-eared copy of my first book, I couldn't have been more flattered. Here's another one for you to scribble in and dog-ear, Marc! I'd also like to thank the team at Intel's Decision Quality office for teaching me something new and for the great discussions. For opening new doors and dragging me through them, I'd like to thank Linda Guariglio and Phillip Smesrud.

I'd like to thank Robert Hutchinson from Apress for believing I had another book cooking in my brain somewhere. He graciously helped me connect a few disjointed ideas into a coherent concept and ultimately into a practical discussion of just how you actually do get started managing a project.

Writing a book is nice challenge, and it really helps when you get to work with rock stars like the folks at Apress. For superbly managing this project, I'd like to thank Rita Fernando. When she started doing "bottoms-up" estimation, I knew right then that she was my kinda PM! I'd also like to thank Matt Moodie for his awesome help cleaning up and sharpening my writing. Of course there are plenty of other hardworking people behind the scenes making this book shine, and I'd like to just say "thanks for making me look good!"

I'd like to thank my family for their continued support and for never once telling me that I was crazy for getting up so early to write. Thanks to Christy Odom and Stormy McBride for providing inspiration for this book; I wrote it for folks like you trying to figure out how to get started on a big project.

Last, my most sincere "thank yous" to all the project teams I've led over the years. Thank you for working so hard and following where I led. I've learned something from each of you and it's truly made me a better project manager.

Introduction

I came to project management as an experienced engineer; I knew how to do my highly technical job and how to get work done within a highly matrixed, international company. What I didn't know was how to perform the basic processes required to manage a project. You see, they seemed so simple as to be completely ignorable, and let's be honest, with a graduate degree in physics, I was arrogant and dismissive. What could be so hard about laying out work on a timeline and calling it the project schedule? I'd like to say that I wised up quickly and realized what I didn't know, but that's not what happened. What happened was about four years of "learning by doing," which really meant "learning while screwing things up." Ironically, it was studying for the Project Management Professional (PMP) certification that woke me up to the best practices for executing some of the processes needed to effectively manage a project. For instance, it turned out that the real reason I had to engage in those epic battles with that popular scheduling software was because I didn't know how to develop a comprehensive schedule in the first place. My frustration wasn't caused by some evil software package; it was caused by my own ignorance. It turns out that there's a very simple, systematic way to collect the information needed to build a good project schedule, and guess what? Once I mastered that method, those epic battles dwindled to the occasional hiccup.

What I learned and, yes, I admit that I learned it the hard way, is that conquering these fundamental processes was a game-changer. Your effectiveness as a PM consists of two equal parts: mastery of these fundamental processes and your agility with interpersonal communication. Trust me, it's significantly harder to improve your soft skills than it is to improve your capability to execute the fundamental processes of project management. These processes are straightforward and easy to grasp, requiring no advanced math and only slightly frightening software applications. The absolute easiest and fastest way to improve as a project manager is to focus on improving your grasp of the mechanics of project management.

This idea that you can dramatically improve your effectiveness by following these best practices is why I wrote this book. These processes are also surprisingly simple to understand. You won't need a semester-long course on scheduling to get started or even to dramatically improve the next schedule you develop. Take the practice of managing project risks. Once you understand that there are really only five options for managing any risk, the hoopla and drama that surround risk management in many organizations boil down to a multiple-choice question.

In all honesty, this should have been my first book. You see, my first book *Managing Projects in the Real World* was all about navigating the people challenges of managing projects. Those are tough challenges, to be sure, but frankly you need to know what the heck you're doing before you can make much headway dealing with a difficult stakeholder or crazy coworker. You really can't respond to that insane request to pull in the schedule by 8 weeks if you don't have a realistic execution plan to start with. In fact, there's a pretty strong case to be made that you should focus on improving your project management mechanics before you deep dive into growing your soft skills.

This book sets up the beginning project manager to do just that with a concise set of instructions and actionable advice on what to do and how to do it. It contains checklists for each phase of the project lifecycle which keep you on track and help you stay organized. The second half of the book is dedicated to how you do this stuff in the Real World, offering advice on how to navigate low and high PM maturity organizations. There are also some actionable ideas for where to go next once you're comfortable with the mechanics of the job. In short, this is the book I wish I'd had when I first started out as a project manager, and I hope it helps those of you out there struggling to master your craft.

Stripping Down Project Management to the Chassis

Congratulations, you're a project manager! Now what do you do?

Project management is a vastly complex and complicated endeavor, and like any other complex and complicated effort it's often hard to know just where to start. In this case it's not that you can't find training material or mentors to help you along your journey, it's that you're completely overwhelmed by all of the information out there and by the consequences of screwing it all up. You feel like you're

Electronic supplementary material The online version of this chapter (doi:10.1007/978-1-4842-2086-3_1) contains supplementary material, which is available to authorized users.

destined to be the featured entrée at a management luau sometime in the distant future if you can't lead this project team. You're completely bewildered by all of the processes you must follow and the documentation you must produce. Never fear! There is a light at the end of this tunnel and this book will help you find it. Now take a deep breath and let's dive right in by stripping down this thing we call project management to the bare bones, the fundamentals, the chassis if you will.

The first thing you need to realize is that the underpinning of all projects is a framework of specific processes that produce the artifacts of project management. Okay, let's stop here for a minute to explain what I mean by the "artifacts of project management." These are the output of those foundational processes and are things like the project schedule, the risk register, the Change Control Board, and the communications plan, to name a few. If you've already acquired your Project Management Professional (PMP) certification, then you already know that there's a whole slew of plans you need to consider as well. The key thing to understand here is that once you master these foundational processes, then your life as a project manager gets a whole lot easier.

Think of this like driving an unfamiliar car. A few years ago, I vacationed in Scotland and I rented a car for transportation. I was able to drive that car because I already knew the sequences and processes for driving an automobile. Get in, put your seatbelt on, get out and switch sides so that you can reach the pedals and steering wheel, seatbelt again, adjust the mirrors, foot on the break, crank the key, engage the clutch, shift into first gear, ease foot onto the gas, and watch out for crazy Yank drivers. You see from this example that I had already mastered the foundational skills for driving, so all I had to concentrate on were the nuances of driving an unfamiliar car in Scotland. Sure, things like driving on the other side of the road gave me a bit of trouble, but I was still able to motor around the Highlands and see that beautiful country. Mastering project management is just like that. Master the fundamentals and you can drive a project anywhere, on either side of the road.

Executing these processes and producing the associated artifacts are what I call the mechanics of project management, and trust me, they aren't that hard to master. Here's the thing: it's not the mechanics that make project management so hard, it's dealing with difficult people that makes it hard. In this book, I'm going to walk you through the mechanics of project management so that when you tackle that next project you can spend more of your time and energy dealing with the people, the really challenging part of project management, instead of struggling through generating the Network Diagram. Oh, and when you're ready to pick up your ball and go to another playground, a.k.a. find another project management job, these foundational skills will enable you to spend more time learning that new organization's politics and nuances because you've got mad skills when it comes to the mechanics of managing a project.

Understanding the Workflow of Any Project

All projects follow the same basic workflow, so you really need to engrain this in your brain. (Figure 1-1) It starts with the Initiating Phase, which we'll discuss in detail in Chapter 2. Essentially, this is where the project objective is determined and the high-level constraints are identified through a process called scoping. It's not uncommon for organizations to have a dedicated team to perform the scoping analysis and provide that to the project manager as a starting place for their work. Next comes the Planning Phase, which we will cover in Chapter 3; this is where the project team develops their overall plan; how they will execute the project, what resources are needed, what the specific deliverables will be, a detailed schedule, etc. Most of the project management processes fall into this phase, and it's where most of the artifacts are developed. In short, Planning is where most of the mechanics of project management occur. It's often considered the most challenging phase of a project to manage, but again, it's not the mechanics of the work that are hard, it's the negotiation and stakeholder management that are hard. Upon exiting the Planning Phase, we will move into the Execution Phase in Chapter 4. This is where the team executes the plan they developed earlier. It goes without saying that the more thorough the planning the smoother the execution. Now, the Project Management Institute (PMI) considers Monitoring and Control to be separate phases but I do not. By the way, PMI is the governing body for the project management profession and they administer a variety of project management certifications including the PMP. The work of Monitoring and Control is basically what you think it is. You monitor the indicators and the project schedule to identify any deviations from the plan. You take steps to control the workflow and progress to continually optimize both. In my opinion, the work of Monitoring and Control happens within the Execution Phase, so it doesn't really warrant its own box in the flow chart, if you know what I mean.

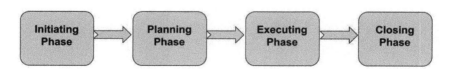

Figure 1-1. Basic project workflow

Now, there's a special set of work that is unique to the Executing Phase, and that's the work you need to do for releasing your project: we'll cover this in Chapter 5. Interestingly, I've found that a lot of great project management training material tends to gloss over the work that needs to happen to launch your project's output, so here I talk about those tricky things like figuring out if you're really ready to release and how to facilitate the final approval meeting.

The last phase is the Closing Phase, which we will cover in Chapter 6; this is where the project team wraps up the work by archiving collateral, dispositioning excess material, performing a retrospective analysis of the project, ensuring long-term support for the project deliverables, reporting out a summary of the project, celebrating their achievements, etc. Closing as you would expect is the end of the road.

As I mentioned, all projects follow the same workflow (Figure 1-2), but how this flow is described or documented varies. This is where the project lifecycle comes in, and there are quite a few of them out there. Your organization will probably expect you to use a specific, well-documented lifecycle, so you don't need to figure out which one to use by yourself. While not exactly the same, all the lifecycles that I've run across have the basic flow I mentioned and many have formal reviews of the deliverables produced during each phase. These reviews are referred to as gate reviews and are often tied to funding and approval for the project team to proceed. You will also run across lifecycles that iterate the basic workflow, such as those following an Agile methodology, where the project team performs smaller, more frequent iterations of the basic flow, combining many iterations to produce the project deliverables one bite at a time.

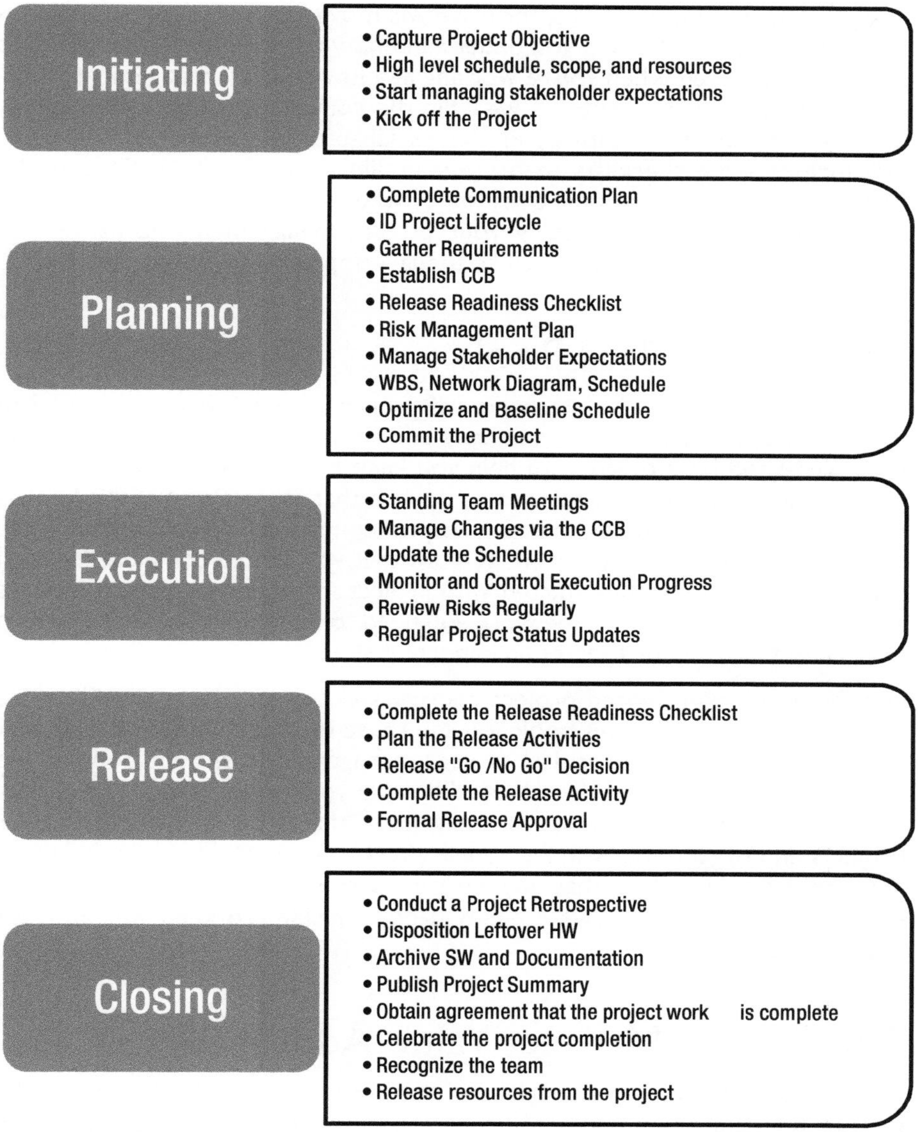

Initiating
- Capture Project Objective
- High level schedule, scope, and resources
- Start managing stakeholder expectations
- Kick off the Project

Planning
- Complete Communication Plan
- ID Project Lifecycle
- Gather Requirements
- Establish CCB
- Release Readiness Checklist
- Risk Management Plan
- Manage Stakeholder Expectations
- WBS, Network Diagram, Schedule
- Optimize and Baseline Schedule
- Commit the Project

Execution
- Standing Team Meetings
- Manage Changes via the CCB
- Update the Schedule
- Monitor and Control Execution Progress
- Review Risks Regularly
- Regular Project Status Updates

Release
- Complete the Release Readiness Checklist
- Plan the Release Activities
- Release "Go /No Go" Decision
- Complete the Release Activity
- Formal Release Approval

Closing
- Conduct a Project Retrospective
- Disposition Leftover HW
- Archive SW and Documentation
- Publish Project Summary
- Obtain agreement that the project work   is complete
- Celebrate the project completion
- Recognize the team
- Release resources from the project

Figure 1-2. The Project Workflow

After we cover Closing in Chapter 6, we will move into some special topics in Part II. In Chapter 7, I'll help you understand how to cherry-pick just the right processes you need when you're working in a low project management maturity organization. For Chapter 8, we'll flip the coin and talk about how to set yourself apart in a high-maturity PM house. Chapter 9 expounds on the sheer brilliance of using checklists to make your life easier. Finally, in Chapter 10, I'll circle back to your original question of where to start by giving you some realistic strategies for improving your project management mechanics and where to go next in your quest to continually improve.

How to Use This Book

The key to mastering the mechanics of project management is to immerse yourself in this workflow and intimately understand the work that happens in each phase and how to do it. To help you keep track of which lifecycle phase you're in and what work remains to be done in that phase, Part I of this book is organized by project phases, and each chapter contains a helpful checklist. These checklists contain the bare minimum work that you should complete for each phase. If you're just getting started with project management, these checklists are a great tool for planning the work you need to do in each phase and to help make sure that you don't forget an important step.

For the more experienced project managers out there, these checklists are your big takeaway from this book. You can reuse the checklists for any project to ensure that all of the critical project management tasks get done at the right point in the project lifecycle. Additionally, you can use them as a springboard to create your own custom checklists that best suit your particular projects and organizations. In fact, these checklists are why I wrote this book. You see, I firmly believe that anyone can master the mechanics of project management, and if you have a handy-dandy checklist to keep you on track you're good to go.

The Project Manager Value-Add

Before we move on to the specifics of the Initiating Phase, I want to spend a few pixels talking about one of the core values a project manager brings to the project team. Yes, as a project manager you're the leader and you bring all of the goodness and responsibility that entails to the team. But really, when you get right down to it, the work a project manager does, the true value-add, is rooted in the mechanics of the job. When you become a project manager, your job is no longer to design the power array or create killer marketing collateral; instead, your job is to develop a realistic execution strategy and plan. It's things like ensuring that real and meaningful risk management plans are developed.

As the project manager, I own the communication to our customers and key stake-holders, not the electrical engineer or the planner, but me, the project manager. Many inexperienced project managers fail to develop their skills in the mechanics of the job because they get consumed by the people challenges. When this hap-pens, things like schedules and strategic communications get de-prioritized and the results are often a project out of control or sinking fast. Project managers must treat these artifacts as key deliverables and hold themselves accountable for developing them on time and with excellent quality. It's quite hypocritical of the project manager to berate a software engineer for a late code drop when they themselves haven't developed a realistic risk management plan. So don't be that PM; instead, spend time with this book and master the mechanics of the job.

Your time will be well spent as your future projects will have more realistic schedules, real risk management plans, solid communication with stakeholders, etc., and all of that leaves you with more time to focus on those stakeholder expectations, strategic partnerships, and, yeah, dealing with those difficult or underperforming team members. One more time with feeling: it's not the mechanics of the job that are hard, it's dealing with demanding people that makes it hard, so master the mechanics and live a happier PM life!

The Mechanics
What to Do and How to Do It

The underpinning of all projects is a framework of specific processes that produce the artifacts of project management. Executing these processes and producing the associated artifacts are what I call the mechanics of project management. Part I takes you through the stripped-down, nuts-and-bolts work you need to do to manage any project. It also contains helpful checklists for each project phase to help you stay on track and keep you from forgetting any of the important bits. Ready to manage a project? Let's get started!

Getting Started on Your First Project

a.k.a. The Initiating Phase

Starting projects can be overwhelming. Where do you start, what exactly do you do first, and who the heck do you need to talk to now versus later? These are just a few of the questions racing through your mind when you get assigned your first project, and it can be pretty overwhelming. You're in the storm path and those swirling, gale-force winds are tugging at your hair but you know that you're just at the edge and that it's gonna get a lot worse before you figure out what the heck you're doing. Welcome to the Initiating Phase of project management! This is real life, where starting a new and complicated endeavor can psych you out. The good news is that most of the time all you've got to do is take that first step and get started. That's what this chapter is all about; getting started.

© Melanie McBride 2016

M. McBride, *Project Management Basics*, DOI 10.1007/978-1-4842-2086-3_2

Initiating

- Capture Project Objective
- High level schedule, scope, and resources
- Start managing stakeholder expectations
- Kick off the Project

Planning

Execution

Release

Closing

A Few Words About Scoping

The scoping activity is precursor to planning, and it's where all of the planning inputs come from; it's also the main work of the Initiating Phase. Here's where the high-level schedule, budget, deliverables, and resources to execute the project are identified.

For the scoping activity, you gather a group of subject matter experts to evaluate the opportunity that is your project and come up with high-level estimates for what's needed to execute the project and a timeline. Often this work is done by a separate team and the project team is provided the output of the scoping analysis to kick off their planning efforts.

Before you get into scoping your new project, you need to understand one thing: scoping is not the same thing as planning, and it requires a completely different mindset. When scoping a project, you need to up-level your thinking. Instead of trying to nail down the specific project requirements, focus your thinking on the big chunks of work. For instance, instead of getting mired in the specifics of the terms and conditions that need to be included in the joint development agreement, simply capture the fact that you need that contract. You and your team will hash out the details of that contract later; the important thing in scoping is to understand the larger deliverables and work packages so that you can come up with a realistic work estimate. Make sense?

As you would expect, some organizations follow a formal scoping process and others wing it. Structured scoping analysis is good; informal scoping is bad. Organizations utilizing a structured scoping process are generally more mature in their overall project management practices and culture. Good scoping involves a systematic examination of the project environment, the market drivers, and the technical feasibility where decisions and project constraints are developed with actual data. If you work in such an organization, then this step of the process is a cakewalk and you take what the scoping team produces and jump right into planning. However, not all of us are so fortunate, so let's talk a bit about how to navigate a less mature organization.

If your organization falls into the informal scoping camp, there are a few things to be aware of. First, it's likely that some aspects of the project environment will be overlooked, as there's no systematic review during the quasi-scoping activity. Project managers should be sure to utilize schedule buffer to deal with factors missed during scoping that can come up during execution. For instance, in some regions extreme weather drives work stoppages, and if this is not accounted for during scoping, there's a good chance that the expected completion date is too aggressive for the project team to hit. A junior project manager might not be aware of the potential work delays due to extreme weather, so if this is missed in scoping, it's likely to be missed during planning as well. A smart PM throws in some schedule buffer to cover these unknown unknowns that come out of half-baked scoping activities.

Another pitfall of informal scoping is the tendency to set project targets based on "gut" feel versus real data. Here's how this goes: the engineering manager asserts that it will only take 3 months to design the controller, so that's the estimate used to determine the expected project completion date. The problem here is that that manager hasn't designed anything in the last 10 years, and the entire design environment is completely different from what he was used to "back in the day." Further, if the project is a high priority for the organization, it's common to see the expected project date set to what the major stakeholders need it to be. This is the target; it's not an actual estimate of the work needed to deliver, and that's a crucial difference. Project managers often feel like this kind of date is "dictated" to them and that the project team must "do whatever it takes" to hit that date. The problem with both of these scenarios is of course that the actual work content is completely ignored in the quasi-analysis. This is actually pretty common in some fields, and project managers need to be on the lookout for this type of informal scoping. During the Planning Phase, the project team will work out what it takes to actually execute the project, and in situations where the scoping was done informally, the project manager will need to educate the stakeholders on this work content as they negotiate the project completion date. Note that if the scoping was done informally, then you should expect to negotiate the project timeline during the planning.

One last pitfall of informal scoping is that you often see internal political motivations driving the scoping analysis. When the project objective is defined, care should be taken that all of the stakeholders agree on what the project should achieve. Often, the project manager will need to bring all parties together and broker a common understanding of the objective and, at a high level, how that objective will be achieved. It's critical to the project's success that this common understanding be developed at this early stage of the project. Yes, you may need to perform this level setting multiple times throughout the project if your organization is particularly unaligned, but at a minimum you should not go into planning with major disconnects among your major stakeholders with respect to what the project should achieve.

Now that you have a good understanding of the scoping activity, let's talk about the specifics of determining the high-level schedule, budget, deliverables, and resources to execute the project; a.k.a. let's scope that project!

Figuring Out the Project Objective

So what's the first step for any project and any project manager, experienced or newbie? It's to figure out what the objective of the project is. Simple, right? Uh huh … Yep, I've been there and this is definitely not simple, so here's what you do. You start asking people, the important people who should know this information. Those "important" people are your stakeholders, and we'll make some sense of them in a bit, so for now just figure out what they think the purpose of the project is. Ask questions like: "*So, Melanie, what do you need this project team to deliver?*" and "*What do you see as the output of this project?*" You know what to do next: ask some confirming questions like "*Okay, so you need us to deliver a new web portal for the POS solution by the end of Q3, correct?*" The objective here is to understand what these VIPs think the project should produce or achieve. At this point in time, you only need that objective, so stay focused and don't get distracted when your stakeholders start moving into solution space or deep-diving into execution strategies. Ignore that noise for now.

Once you've talked to several people and you feel like you have a handle on what they want you to do, write it down. Yes, really, write or type that objective out. There's a really good reason for taking this step and it's to test your understanding of the goal of the project. You should be able to state the objective in one succinct sentence. If you can't clearly articulate this, then you don't know enough about the project yet; go talk to more "important" people. Notice the confirming question above; in that example the project objective is to deliver a web portal to support the Point Of Sale solution by the end of the 3rd fiscal quarter. This concise statement is your starting point and touchstone for the rest of the project, so it makes sense to start here, doesn't it?

Figure Out Who the Major Stakeholders Are ... and Go Talk to Them

Now that you've got a project objective, you're ready to start identifying those stakeholders. For now, you're only going to focus on the major ones, and we'll come back to building out a complete stakeholder list later. This will be the start of your stakeholder management plan, so it's time to capture some data; for this, I generally use Excel, but you can use whatever application floats your boat. Start by making a list of the people within your organization that care about this project. For now, just focus on the most influential and the decision-makers. Capture each person's role and what they care about with respect to the project. Now go talk to each one and discuss what they see as the project objective and what the project success criteria are. You want to confirm your understanding of the project objectives and what constitutes success, and start building collaborative relationships with these stakeholders. Yes, this is going to take some time, and yes, you really have to talk to these people. A big part of project management, you will find, is relationship building, so even if you think you know what the objective is, make that appointment and start building relationships with those key stakeholders, 'cause trust me, you're gonna need them later!

Figure Out the High-Level Project Constraints: The Triple Constraint

At this point, you should have a solid project objective and a pretty good idea of who the major stakeholders are, so it's time to figure out the high-level project constraints. Once upon a time in a land far, far away, project managers worshiped at the altar of the venerable Triple Constraint. Time passed, and the empire that is PMI moved away from this construct in favor of other ideas; however, those of us who were chiseling out project schedules with rocks still recall and use the Triple Constraint.

The Triple Constraint is a construct that defines the relationship of the schedule, scope, and resources of a project. Think of it as a triangle, one where the legs represent the available resources, the expected completion date or schedule, and the scope of work. (Figure 2-1) The idea here is that the integrity of the triangle must be maintained, so if the schedule is pulled in, that is, if the schedule leg of the triangle is shortened, then to maintain the integrity of the triangle the resources leg, the scope leg, or both must change as a result of shortening the schedule leg. It works like this: if you want to pull in the schedule then you need to either add more people to do the work (elongate the resources leg) or reduce the scope of work (shorten the scope leg). To maintain the triangle you must change one of the other two legs if you want to shorten the schedule leg. That's it; there's no free lunch here, folks. This construct still informs my thinking when I'm looking at changes to the project environment, and I use it regularly to help illustrate just why it is that my project team can't pull in the schedule without affecting anything else. Okay, enough of the history lesson; let's get on to figuring out the high-level project constraints!

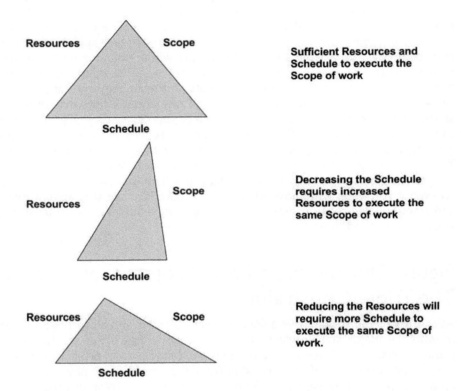

Figure 2-1. Triple Constraint

The High-Level Schedule

Generally, there are only two things you need to figure out with respect to the project schedule at this point in the project: the expected end date and any interim deliverables the team must meet. This part is actually pretty easy if you keep in mind that you're doing this analysis from a bigger-picture view of the project. The goal here is to figure out when those major stakeholders expect your team to wrap up the project, and trust me, they all have a clear idea of what that date should be. Whether or not the date is realistic is another issue, and you'll tackle it during planning. Think of this date as a target, NOT a commitment; though it may be presented as a dictate, it's always negotiable later during the Planning Phase. One pitfall junior project managers fall into here is the expectation that this date is set in stone and there's no wiggle room for reality. In fact, that date is often fixed for very good business reasons, and okay, for some not-so-good wishful-thinking reasons. However, that doesn't mean that other things like the scope of work, the budget, and the resources are not negotiable. So for now, don't get too wrapped around the axle on this date: it's a target only. Don't let your team lose focus or get distracted by a blatantly unrealistic date; instead, keep them focused on gathering data to understand the problem that they need to solve with this project.

Now don't forget to discuss those interim deliverables with your major stakeholders as well. Often there are commitments made, or expectations set, for test material, mock-ups, sample output, test results, etc., to other parties. These committed dates need to feed into the team's planning process, so you need to uncover them early. Just like that "target" completion date, consider these dates to be targets where your team will assess their ability to hit those targets during planning. Yes, folks, at this stage of a project all deliverables and their associated dates are negotiable; the trick though is to wait until you've done some planning before renegotiating them. At this stage of the game, all you've got are those hysterical voices in your head telling you that there's no way the team can hit that deliverable on time. This isn't a strong negotiation position for you. However, if you wait a bit until some of the planning is done, then you can offer up alternatives with business impacts based on data. Once you've got options and the cost of those options in your back pocket, you can renegotiate the schedule, scope, and resources required to execute the project from a position of strength. Therefore, don't burn your political capital trying to weasel out of an unrealistic date at this stage. Sure, it's okay to express doubt about the team's ability to perform such a miracle, but be sure to emphasize that your team will "crunch the numbers" and come back with some viable options for those major stakeholders to consider. Those stakeholders purely love to "consider options" and make prioritization calls, and you're going to provide the data for them to do just that during planning, so don't spend your energy fighting with these folks now: you've got better things to do, like finishing the scoping work.

The High-Level Scope of Work

You've probably caught on by now to the fact that when you are meeting with these major stakeholders, you're going to talk about more than just the objective of the project. In fact, you'll cover the objective plus the Triple Constraint components, schedule, scope, and resources, so now let's break down what you need to figure out with respect to the high-level scope of work for the project. You need to determine the big pieces of functionality that the project needs to deliver. These items will turn out to be the most important deliverables from your stakeholder's perspective, so you need to spend some time talking about how each stakeholder views the project deliverables and what aspects of the project are important to each stakeholder. This is only the beginning of requirements gathering, and it's likely that these major stakeholders don't know or particularly care about the specific details. Instead, they tell you that they want your team to develop that web portal. The specifics of that portal's design will be developed during requirements gathering in the Planning Phase. Basically you want to answer the "is it bigger than a breadbox or smaller than a matchbook" question with respect to the scope of work. Be careful to separate the deliverable from the solution or how stakeholders expect the team to execute the project. Often, these major stakeholders have strong opinions in this space, but keep in mind that things like the use of specific software applications, project methodologies, and/or design practices are not scope. Smile and nod when these things come up and commit the team to evaluating these ideas during planning.

The High-Level Resources

Now we come to the tricky topic of resources for your new project. Here you need to understand which of your major stakeholders are funding the project and what aspects of the project each stakeholder is funding. The basic question is: what is this project expected to cost? Trust me when I say that each of these stakeholders has a dollar amount in mind and it may or may not be grounded in the reality of previous project budgets. Just like discussing the delivery date and the scope of work, keep in mind that you're simply collecting data at this point, so gather those stakeholder expectations and know that you will probably need to renegotiate budget once the team has figured out the requirements and execution strategy. You also need to be aware of the fact that not all costs fall into the same financial buckets. This is specific to each company and organization, so spend some time reviewing the budget for a previous project with an experienced colleague so that you get a feel for what those buckets are and any accounting nuances you need to be aware of. For instance, travel costs are a big "gotcha" for a lot of project teams. The travel budget may come from the program or project bucket or it can come from the reporting structure for each team member. If your project will require team members to travel, especially internationally, then you need to understand where the money to pay for that travel will come from and what the expected cost of that travel is. The last thing you want to hear midway through the Execution Phase is that a critical engineer can't travel to an important customer site for a demo because her department doesn't have the travel budget to cover the cost. Don't forget to consider the team size and location, since these factors also affect projected travel costs.

Speaking of team size and location, be sure to discuss these two factors with your major stakeholders too. Has it been decided already that the Poland team will develop the cloud infrastructure while the India team develops the software? What about the facilities your team will need? Will the team be working with the previous ad agency in San Francisco? If so, do they need some office space there? Often, junior project managers find that these kinds of decisions are already made prior to kicking off the project, so you need to understand them before moving into the Planning Phase. Let me give you an example of what I'm talking about here. Once I had a project where it was decided that the team would do the power-on testing of the new design in one of the company's facilities in California. That decision was made without me in the loop. Unfortunately, this CA lab consisted of one borrowed work bench in some other organization's lab. Therefore, our project plan had to include the work to build up the lab infrastructure to support the testing we needed to do. If I'd asked my major stakeholders about resources and team locations during the Initiating Phase of the project, I probably could have changed that decision to use a nonexistent lab. Instead, my team and I had to do extra work to accommodate this little surprise later in the project. So learn from my mistake and be sure to discuss how many team members your stakeholders expect you to need and where the work will be done now rather than waiting for an unpleasant surprise later.

Another key question you need to ask is this: has the project team already been identified? In organizations with mature project management practices, the answer is usually "no," but in reality, this assignment of resources often happens much sooner, so it's a good idea to understand who's already tagged to work on the project at this stage of the game. If the project team has not been assigned yet, then you have an opportunity to influence who will be selected. Ask yourself who you'd like to be on the team based on the skills you think you'll need, technical expertise, ability to work well with a team, etc. Also consider potential team members you do not want added to the team. It doesn't hurt to lobby for those key team members early, so don't miss the opportunity to do so before resources are assigned. The best practice is to wait until the Planning Phase to pull the team together after you've identified the skill sets needed to execute the project, but in reality much of the team is already assigned to the project before the Planning Phase starts.

Figure Out the Players

By this point in your work, you've probably made several additions to your list of major stakeholders, so it's time to build out a stakeholder management tool. The idea here is to build a list of people who have an interest in your project. You will use this list later in planning, and it will be one of the most useful tools you develop to manage your project, so invest the time now to build out a list of players. You can use any software application you like, and I tend to toggle between a spreadsheet and a mind map depending on which tools I'm using to manage the project.

To start, make a list of all of the people involved in, influenced by, or affected by your project. Who's got "some skin in the game"? Who are your customers and partners? Who are the likely project saboteurs? This should be a long list, and it will grow as the project evolves. For each person, capture their organization, their role with respect to the project, their location and time zone, and their contact information. All of these people are your stakeholders, since at some level they can influence the project direction. During the Planning Phase, you will use this list to develop your project communication plan, so yes, be sure to capture that location and time zone info while you're already looking up reporting structures and job roles.

Now that you've got a solid list of stakeholders, it's time to refine it and identify the key project stakeholders. Here you want to identify those people who are decision-makers, budget owners, highly influential players, project approvers, etc.: basically those people who can shut down or completely derail the project. These are your key stakeholders, and during planning you will also develop a stakeholder management plan.

Building the Project Charter

Now that you've met with the major stakeholders and have a pretty good idea of the project objective and the high-level project constraints, it's time to build a project charter. The charter is a document that basically captures the information you've been gathering informally. There are two camps when it comes to the importance and ownership of a project charter, so let me explain.

The first camp is the Project Management Institute (PMI), the organization that governs the project management profession. PMI maintains a documented set of best practices for managing projects and programs called the Project Management Body of Knowledge (PMBOK) which is available for purchase (nonmembers) or download (members) from their website, www.pmi.org. The PMBOK is considered the definitive word on the work of project management. According to the PMBOK, the project charter is solely owned by the project sponsor, and it specifically authorizes the project manager to utilize resources to execute the project. Further, the charter outlines such things as the business need the project is expected to fulfill, the high-level requirements, assumptions, and constraints, the schedule milestones, the budget, the stakeholders, etc. As you would expect, such a document is held in high regard and considered very important by PMI. In short, it's everything a project manager needs to know to get started all delivered with a big glittery bow.

That's what PMI thinks; now let me explain the other camp when it comes to project charters. For many of us, myself included, the project charter is like that mythical unicorn; everyone knows what it looks like, yet no one has actually seen one! I've never found a project charter to be all that helpful, mostly because I've never been given one at the beginning of a project. I have completed a charter template and posted it to a project repository then promptly forgot about it for the rest of the project, so you could say that I've used them but that's a pretty liberal interpretation of what I actually did. Often, your organization's Project Management Office (PMO) will require a project charter, and you will be expected to comply with their expectation that a charter exists. However, the PMO mandates do not mean that there are formal project sponsors assigned or that these sponsors will actually do the work to develop a fully documented charter. In my opinion, the charter is pretty useless to a project manager. First, if I happen to get lucky and am handed a charter that a project sponsor or scoping team developed, I'm still going to validate the information with each of the major stakeholders. This information is too important to the Planning Phase to get wrong and I sure don't want to find out that there's a disconnect between major stakeholders about a key deliverable once the team has started the Execution Phase. Second, if I'm not lucky and I have to create the charter myself, then it's duplicate work for me, as all of that information is contained in my project plan. So I'm going to do the informational interviews with the major stakeholders anyway, and I'm going to document the critical information in my project plan, which is then reviewed by said stakeholders at the end of the Planning Phase, so I really don't see any value in a project charter.

As has been mentioned, the charter *should* be provided to the project manager at the initiation of the project. The project sponsor *should* own this document and it *should* reflect the output of a scoping analysis. The reality is that there are an awful lot of *shoulds* that never actually happen in the real world, so if your organization requires a project charter, then this is the point in the project timeline where it makes its appearance and either you or the project sponsor *should* put it together. I've shared my experience with you but your organization may handle project charters in a different manner, so do what you need to in order to stay on the right side of the PMO and continue to make progress on defining the project.

Holding the Project Kick-Off Meeting

Okay, you are now ready to hold the project kick-off meeting! This is for many of your team members and stakeholders the official start of the project. Before you schedule this important meeting, there are a few key considerations to think about. What kind of team dynamic do you need for this project? Is this going to be a "pedal to the metal," "no holds barred" screamer of a project where speed of execution trumps everything? Or is this a lower-priority project with a limited budget, where ingenuity and innovation will determine whether or not the team is successful? Each team needs a different dynamic, and setting the stage for a team that has a refined sense of urgency or an open collaborative approach starts with the kick-off meeting. Think about what traits you need to incentivize and foster when setting up this first team meeting. If you want to set the stage for a high-performing team, then now's the time to do it. Consider how you will communicate the project objectives and high-level constraints to your teammates. Is this information something you need to send out ahead of the meeting so that the team members can review it and come with any questions? What about your expectations of the team and the "rules of the road" you will all live by for the duration of the project? If you expect team members to let you know if they can't make a meeting ahead of time, then you need to explicitly state that during the kick-off meeting. Be sure to consider and include how the team will be governed. Which decision-making method will you use, and how will meeting agendas be set? The kick-off meeting needs to go well, and everyone needs to feel included right out of the gate, so take the time to properly prepare for this important meeting.

■ **Note** It's extremely important to specifically state any team governance items during the project kick-off meeting. As I mentioned, you can't hold your teammates accountable if you haven't broken down the rules of the road to them. To get you started, consider including these items in your kick-off material: expectations for attending meetings and notification practices if a team member can't attend; expectations of mutual trust and respect; that everyone is expected to speak up and participate in the meeting; that team members will share potential roadblocks and showstoppers early to avoid surprises; that everyone on the team succeeds or fails together, etc.

Checklist #1—Initiating Phase

The Initiating Phase of the project is where it all starts. Key information is gathered, scoping is performed, and the project kick-off meeting is conducted. Complete these major tasks and you are ready to enter the project's Planning Phase. These items are arranged in chronological order, but note that you may end up completing them in any order; the important thing is to do them all before proceeding to the next phase of the project.

Checklist #1—The Initiating Phase

☐ Capture the objective of the project in 1 complete, succinct sentence

☐ High-level project schedule milestones identified

☐ High-level scope of work identified

☐ High-level project resources (budget and people) identified

☐ 1st draft of the stakeholder management tool developed

☐ Complete the project charter (if needed)

☐ Hold the project kick-off meeting

Congratulations! You've just exited the Initiating Phase of your project! See, that wasn't so hard, was it? Now let's move on to Planning and have some real fun!

Doin' Work

a.k.a. The Planning Phase

If you've completed Checklist #1, and the kick-off meeting happened last week, it's time to start doin' the hard work of planning the project. For many project managers, the Planning Phase is the most difficult. This is where the bulk of the mechanics will be done and it's also where you encounter your first, and most serious, soft skill challenges. The good news, as I mentioned in Chapter 1, is that once you master the mechanics you'll have more energy and time to focus on those more difficult challenges, so let's get started, shall we?

© Melanie McBride 2016
M. McBride, *Project Management Basics*, DOI 10.1007/978-1-4842-2086-3_3

Initiating

Planning

- •Complete Communication Plan
- •ID Project Lifecycle
- •Gather Requirements
- •Establish CCB
- •Release Readiness Checklist
- •Risk Management Plan
- •Manage Stakeholder Expectations
- •WBS, Network Diagram, Schedule
- •Optimize and Baseline Schedule
- •Commit the Project

Execution

Release

Closing

Determining the Project Lifecycle

The first thing you've got to decide is which project lifecycle or methodology best suits your project. This is no more than a framework that defines the specific stages of the project work. It is well understood by the organization and the various team members. The most common project lifecycle models are Waterfall, Agile, and Theory of Constraints (TOC), and each has particular strengths. It's quite common for an organization to have resources set up in support of, and a cultural bias toward, a particular lifecycle. If that's your world, then you really don't have anything to decide; just go with what's already established. Whew, one less decision to make! However, if your organization doesn't have expectations, then you can certainly choose the lifecycle model that best fits your project, so let's break down the top three.

WHAT'S ALL THE DRAMA ABOUT ANYWAY?

Interestingly, this is one of those areas of project management where there's a lot of intellectual drama around which lifecycle is the best. Note that this assumes that there really is one "best" model that will work for all projects, which even a novice project manager can tell you is unrealistic. The top three all have their proponents, and these folks are quite passionate about their favorites. Personally, I don't get it; it's a tool, not a cure-all. You see, many people associate organizational and cultural deficiencies with the project execution methodology. The thinking goes something like this: *We can't fully define the requirements during planning so that's why Waterfall fails and it's also why Agile is the best way to go.* This argument fails to hold water, in my opinion, because in most instances the project team could have defined the requirements if they had gone about collecting them in a systematic manner.

Think of it this way. These project lifecycles are simply tools the project team uses to guide their work. If you need to remove a dead tree from your front yard, you have a number of tools to choose from. You could nibble away at that monster live oak with a limb saw but it would take you a really long time. You could also fire up that chainsaw collecting dust in your garage and go at it like a wild man. But let's say you've still got some common sense and that's a really big tree, so you whip out your wallet and pay a professional to remove the tree. Note that the objective here is to remove the tree, not to use the chainsaw: all too often, we dictate a project methodology thinking that it will improve project execution when it's simply the wrong tool for the job. In fact, I think that the real problems are cultural. Remember, tool selection doesn't fix a broken culture and you can't blame a framework for crappy execution.

Waterfall Project Lifecycle

The Waterfall lifecycle is probably the most common and widely used project lifecycle model. The Project Management Institute (PMI) has a rich history with this framework, and their PM Body of Knowledge (PMBOK) is primarily based on it. If you've attained your Project Management Professional (PMP) certification, then you're already well aware of the ins and outs of Waterfall. It's a phased approach to project execution with gate reviews at the end of each phase. The most commonly used project scheduling software, Microsoft Project, is optimized first and foremost for the Waterfall lifecycle. It should be noted that the thoroughness of planning is a critical success factor for projects following this lifecycle. With this one, failing to plan is truly planning to fail, and that's what makes this lifecycle so challenging for junior project managers who may not yet have a feel for what it takes to adequately plan a project.

The Waterfall methodology works well when the requirements can be adequately defined. Note that this requires a systematic approach to requirements gathering that many project teams skim over. This methodology also works well when the team has to incorporate many interdependent deliverables into the project. Scheduling software packages that support Waterfall are often exquisitely optimized to handle these interdependent work packages, but they do require a skilled user to construct this type of schedule. Waterfall works best for midsized projects lasting several quarters to a year with less than twenty discrete resources to track. Finally, the most important reason to utilize the Waterfall lifecycle is its superior ability to predict the project milestones and ultimately the completion date.

Waterfall doesn't work well when the requirements are ambiguous or changing frequently, since the all of the planning work is done up front. This model also flounders when the customer doesn't know what they want and project success depends on innovative customer experiences, since there's not a customer feedback loop built into the lifecycle. Trying to plan a long-term project with many resources and complicated interdependencies, using Waterfall, becomes a frustrating exercise in complexity. The biggest problem with Waterfall is that when the lifecycle fails, it tends to fail epically. When things go south, it's often noticed late in the project execution and there's a substantial amount of sunk cost incurred. Worse, it's entirely possible to execute flawlessly and still deliver something the customer doesn't like or won't use with this methodology. In short, the Waterfall methodology has little tolerance for inadequate project planning.

Agile Methodology

The Agile methodology is something entirely different from Waterfall. It's a framework of iterative execution; each iteration consists of planning, execution, and release. Think of this one as the "lather-rinse-repeat" mode of project execution. While there are many different software packages to choose from, two of the most popular are JIRA and Rally. Here team members self-organize to meet specific project needs and deadlines. Primarily used for software development, this methodology is particularly useful when the user experience is paramount to the project's success. Unlike Waterfall where all of the requirements must be documented up front and with good detail, the Agile method focuses on sufficient documentation at each iteration, thereby giving the team the ability of take advantage of, and react to, changing requirements. It should be noted that it's very challenging to get this one right unless the organization already knows and loves Agile.

Agile is often the best tool for software development and in instances where the customer doesn't know what they want or can't articulate the specifics of the final deliverable. Teams find Agile useful in rapid prototyping scenarios or for projects involving iterative design strategies. It excels at delivering on-target user experiences. Agile also works well with truly multidisciplinary teams where each team member can fill many of the roles needed to execute the project. Because this methodology is so different from the more traditional Waterfall lifecycle, it most successful when the organization understands and embraces the Agile mindset.

The Agile methodology doesn't fare well in a predominantly Waterfall culture, where the management mindset is focused on specific milestones and deliverables. Due to the iterative nature of this framework, the project team cannot commit to deliver the full set of features required by a specific date. They can, and do, commit to deliver the most important features on that specific date, but again, due to the cyclical nature of Agile planning, a high-confidence commitment is not possible during the early stages of the project. Whether or not that is acceptable to the management chain is the Achilles heel of this methodology. This methodology also breaks down for teams where each member can only fill one specialized role, such as that of a database analyst or web designer. The flexibility of the project team to react to the changing development environment is a true advantage of the Agile lifecycle; however, if the team itself doesn't have the necessary technical flexibility to react quickly, this advantage is lost. Finally, if there is no Agile infrastructure present, I strongly suggest you leave this one alone. It's too big of a hurdle for a junior project manager to implement a radically different lifecycle framework for your first project. You need to pick your battles, and cultural issues shouldn't be your focus for your first few projects.

TOC Lifecycle Model

The TOC methodology is similar to Waterfall but with the use of systematic/ strategic buffering. Each major milestone, or work package, has a carefully calculated schedule buffer associated with it. Tasks are planned at 60–80% confidence durations; then, a buffer is added to the endpoint milestone. The project manager manages the buffer consumption, not the specific work packages, and commits are communicated as a confidence range (low, medium, high). The idea is to optimize the workflow through the critical chain, and whether or not specific work packages are completed on time is not so important. This methodology is better than Waterfall at dealing with complicated interdependent work packages/deliverables. ProChain is a commonly used software package associated with TOC, and with the exception of how the buffers are managed, it looks and feels very much like Microsoft Project.

TOC works well when the project environment is particularly ambiguous and the predictability of the completion date is important. Because it is a tweak of the Waterfall methodology, it works well in environments where Waterfall flourishes, such as those in which requirements can be adequately defined and in which there are a lot of complicated interdependencies. TOC does well in organizations with mature project management practices. Further, unlike Agile, it's much easier to switch to TOC if you are already working in a Waterfall-oriented culture.

TOC struggles in organizations where schedule buffers are considered "padding" and the management tolerance for commit windows is low. It also suffers the same weaknesses discussed above for the Waterfall lifecycle. Last, TOC is difficult to practice in organizations where the management focus on specific deliverables trumps achieving the project milestones. This is a subtle but important point. Recall that with a TOC schedule, each deliverable is scheduled with a 60–80% confidence duration, making it highly unlikely that all deliverables will be completed on time. In organizations where team members are rigidly held to hit deliverable due dates, this creates a no-win situation for the project team and leads to inflated work estimates, with baked-in buffers. The end result is a team that is viewed as underperforming with a project schedule containing an overly large amount of buffer.

There you go: the pros and cons of the top three project lifecycles. As I mentioned, if this is one of your first projects, then pick the lifecycle that your team and management chain already understand. It's too big of a hurdle to try to change an organization's culture while figuring out the nuances of how to lead a project team. Save that dogfight for another time once you've mastered the mechanics of project management. Still not sure which one to go with? Pick the Waterfall methodology simply because this book follows it and I'll virtually hold your hand while you grind through the mechanics.

Setting Up Your Team

Okay, it's now time to start revving up your project team, so let's get started. You've already held the kick-off meeting, so there are a few things you need to do right away. The first thing you need to do is schedule regular, recurring team meetings. Now at first blush, you'd think that would be easy, wouldn't you? Not so, my friend, not so. You need to do some planning before hitting send on that calendar invite. First, consider who's on the team and where in the world they are located. Pick a time that best suits all of your team members, a time that falls into normal working hours for each person. Project managers leading geo-dispersed teams already know that this can be challenging. If you can't find a time that is reasonable for everyone, then set up a rotating meeting schedule so that no one geography gets slighted. Yes, this is more work for you, and yes, you'll need to put a bit more effort into "reminding" team members when the next meeting will be held, but this one consideration goes a long, long way to building a high-performing team. After you figure out a good timeslot it's time to turn your attention to the standing meeting agenda. I find that an agenda that includes time to review change requests (more on this later), individual team member updates, opens, and action items works well for most project teams. Obviously, you also need to book a conference room if your team will be meeting face to face or set up a teleconference if your team is spread around the world. It's a good practice to book these meetings out for a few weeks past the expected project completion date, because the team will need to wrap up loose ends and do the work of closing the project after the release date.

Now that you've got all those meetings organized, there are a few more house-keeping tasks to take care of. Often, you will need to set up new accounts and update your organization's tool(s) of record for tracking your project work, including financial, project metric, and resource-tracking systems. Since these tools are specific to your organization, I can't help you here, but I suspect you've got more help in this space than you need from your colleagues in charge of those systems. If you haven't already done so, then you also need to set up a project repository. This is a specific place where all of the project documents will reside while they are being developed. Many organizations use Microsoft SharePoint or some other document repository for this pur-pose. Okay, one last housekeeping task to take care of: collect your team-mate's vacation and training plans for the expected duration of the project. Put another way, send your team an e-mail asking them to provide any dates they will not be available to work on the project for the specific time period you expect the project to run. You will need this information when you build the project schedule later.

Develop a Communication Plan

The next step in our planning process is to develop a communication plan; it's quick to do and will prove extremely useful throughout the life of the project. A communication plan outlines how you will communicate important project information to your team and your stakeholders. It's often just a simple one-page document that outlines how project status, major decisions, upcoming changes, and escalations will be communicated and who these things will be communicated to. To build this plan, first start with the stakeholder manage-ment plan you built in Chapter 2. Remember that Excel spreadsheet that listed each stakeholder and what they cared about? If you were paying atten-tion, then you also thought to capture where these folks work, and if you were really on your A game, then you thought to ask the key stakeholders how they preferred to get updates. If you didn't catch their preferred communication method, then go find that out now so that you can figure out the best way to communicate your project status updates. To create the communication plan, I will often use a second worksheet in my stakeholder management plan to capture this information. First, list all of the major project communication opportunities such as project status updates, reporting out test results, com-municating changes to the scope of work, etc. Then, identify who needs this information. Next, determine how frequently this information needs to be sent out. For instance, there should be a line item for project status informa-tion, it should go to all stakeholders, and it should go out on a regular basis. If there's a required format for this information, note that as well and perhaps include a hyperlink to a required web tool so that all of your communications information is located in one spreadsheet. Once you've completed the plan for all important project information, take the opportunity to sit down with each of your major stakeholders and review your plan to make sure that it meets their expectations and needs. In a perfect world, you would only need to send out one project status update in a format that is easiest for you to update. In the real world, it's often prudent to send out an up-leveled update to your key stakeholders to ensure that they are getting the information they need and to actively manage their expectations with respect to the team's progress. That's all there is to a communication plan: see, I told you it was quick!

Facilitate the Collection of Requirements

Now we're moving into the belly of the beast and starting to get some serious PM work going; the next step is to facilitate the collection of requirements. If you're feeling a tad overwhelmed at this point, don't worry: that's completely normal. Requirements gathering is second only to the angst of dealing with the stakeholders' expected completion date for generating drama and PM stress. Hang in there and I'll walk you through this snake pit.

The process of gathering requirements is actually pretty simple. Here's a perfect example of the mechanics being simple while the people aspects are hard. This is how it works in a nutshell. The technical lead, the business analyst, or whoever is leading the requirements gathering process meets with the appropriate stakeholders and collects their wants and desires with respect to the project output. Please note that it is not the project manager who generally leads the requirements gathering. These requirements are then documented in some form or fashion depending on the organization, usually in a specification or product requirements document. After the technical lead is satisfied with the completeness of the set of requirements, the team does a detailed review of the requirements, making adjustments as needed along the way. After the requirements have been updated with the review feedback, they are considered "frozen" and any further changes require a formal change request. Simple, right? Well, I did say that it was the people that make this part so challenging, didn't I?

The first thing you need to understand about requirements gathering is the role of the project manager in this process. It's not what you think it is and it's not what you've done in the past as a team member. The job of the project manager is to ensure that due diligence was done in the requirements gathering and that all affected functional areas are represented in the process. In general, the technical lead for your project will conduct the requirements gathering; you as the PM need to orchestrate the process of collecting and reviewing them. Further, during the requirements review process you need to keep your PM hat firmly on. You are no longer a part of the team for your technical prowess; instead, you're there to provide leadership and organization. This is a big distinction, and many new PMs struggle to separate these two very different perspectives when leading their first few projects.

Okay, so what should a project manager be doing during requirements gathering? First off, you need to ensure that this work is completed in a timely manner, so set an expected completion date and make it a tad aggressive. The goal here is to drive a sense of urgency but not contribute to the already amped-up atmosphere that is common during requirements collection. It's important that the PM hold the entire team to completing the requirements collection by a specific date because, if left to their own devices, your team-mates will stall out here, overcome with analysis paralysis. During this work, you should expect to step in and facilitate discussions about specific require-ments, negotiating with key stakeholders as necessary to assist the technical lead. After the requirements are gathered, the team will then move into a peer review process. While reviewing the requirements, keep in mind that you're not a technical reviewer; instead, you need to consider things like complete-ness, testability, and whether or not the needs of each affected functional area are captured. Whenever I need to review requirements from both the technical and the project management perspectives, I find it easier to do two separate reviews so that I look at the requirements from the appropriate mindset each time. After the review is completed, the PM needs to ensure that all parties agree that the requirements are accurate and in sufficient detail to inform the project work. This agreement needs to be formally documented and stored as part of the project documentation archive. Once that agree-ment has been reached, communicate that the requirements are frozen and any changes must be approved by the project Change Control Board.

Obviously, I'm skimming the highpoints of requirements collection here. The important thing to keep in mind is the role of the project manager. Your job is to make sure that this process happens in a timely and comprehensive man-ner and that all affected parties are in agreement about the requirements. I mentioned that you want to drive a sense of urgency but in reality, your team needs to take as much time as is needed to get the requirements right. The requirements are the core of the project work and the time you save by accepting half-baked requirements is dwarfed by the amount of time you will spend rehashing the definition and implementation of those requirements later. The time a team takes in requirements gathering is a bit of a balancing act, and while it may seem murky to you now, as you gain experience as a proj-ect manager you will develop a sense for how long this process should take. For now, set a reasonable target date for completing the process, then push it out if the team truly needs more time to get it right. You can always make up schedule with solid requirements, but you will likely go slower if the require-ments are vague, missing, or in contention. Think of this as a "pay me now, or pay me later" scenario and take enough time to develop solid requirements. Last, if you get tagged to also lead the requirements collection efforts, then I highly encourage you to do some research into this process. There's a lot of great training material out there on how to plan for, write, and collect good requirements. I personally find it distracting and difficult to do both require-ments collection and manage the overall project, so if you find yourself in that predicament, I strongly encourage you to find a mentor and a colleague who can help you out here.

Establish the Project Change Control Board

If you recall, we said that once everyone buys off on the requirements all changes need to be approved by the project Change Control Board. Now's the time to set that up! The first thing you need to do is to determine how changes will be tracked, reviewed, and approved: what process will you use? Remember that here you're only concerned about changes that are internal to your project team, so you don't need a wildly complicated process or massive approval board. Here's my recommendation: dedicate 10–15 minutes at the start of each team meeting to the project CCB. During that time, review any new changes and discuss them as a team, then document the outcome of that discussion in the meeting minutes. During that discussion, your team will determine what you're going to do about that request, so you need to determine who will be a voting member of the CCB, that is, who can approve or deny the request. For my project teams, the voting members—in fact, all of the members of the CCB—are the project team, and we follow the decision-making process we all agreed to in the kick-off meeting. Independent of the meeting minutes, you need to record change requests into a Change Control Log so that you have a history of changes and why those changes were made. This log is extremely useful when closing the project to summarize everything that went on, so it pays to take the time to set up that log now.

That's the overall process for tracking changes internally, but there are a few details you need to take care of as the PM. First, you need to determine which types of changes must be reviewed by the CCB. A good rule of thumb is that a change request must be submitted for any change that modifies the form, fit, or function of the project deliverable. You also need to create a change request form and distribute it to the team for use. This form should collect all of the information the team needs to evaluate a potential change, including what is changing, why the change is needed, what's affected by the change, and how long this change will take to implement by functional area. Along with the specifics of the change, your form should also include space to document the change submitter, how the request is dispositioned (approved, conditionally approved, denied, etc.), the date the change is dispositioned, the total schedule impact of the change, and any relevant details to the implementation of the change (revision changes, implementation date, etc.). This can be a simple form that you create in whatever software application you like. Finally, you need to determine who needs to be advised of any project CCB decisions and how you will communicate those changes to them. This can be as simple as information captured in meeting minutes or it may require a separate communication to key stakeholders. The whole point here is that the project team CCB should be as simple and painless as possible so that your teammates will actually use it.

Ah, I know what you're thinking now: Change Control Boards are scary and the whole process is Byzantine, right? Well they can be at the organization level, but at the project level they can and should be simple, short, and sweet.

For the project team CCB, I view this process more as a communication tool rather than a gauntlet to run. The goal here is to make it as easy as possible for your team to talk about changes in a way that includes everyone affected. This is a critical process, so you really need to set it up in such a way that it works for your team. Those organizational CCBs are another matter entirely, and we will talk more about them in Chapter 4 during the Execution Phase.

Identifying Organizational Project Management Requirements

Now that you've got the framework of your project execution process defined, it's time to start bolting on some parts. In this case I'm talking about any specific organizational requirements for your project artifacts. Just like in scoping, some organizations are more mature in their project management practices than others. If you work in an organization that can't spell "project management" without a dictionary, then chances are the expectations about what project management artifacts you produce are pretty low. This actually makes the job of a junior project manager harder, because it can be confusing determining what you really need. If that's where you're at, then just follow this book and produce the artifacts we walk through. You don't need to do anything else. If however, you work in an organization with a Project Management Office (PMO), then the chances are good that you are expected to produce specific documents in specific formats. My rule of thumb is that no matter what format I am required to use, I focus primarily on those that help me actually manage the project. All of the other bureaucratic detritus I put as little effort into as I can get away with. Let me give you an example of what I'm talking about here. I once worked in an organization where I was required to use a specific change request form. The problem, as you can probably guess, was that the form had a ton of fields for the change request submitter to fill out that were not relevant to evaluating the impact of a proposed change. What happens when you try to get your teammates to use a confusing, overly complicated form? No one uses it, that's what! My teammates were simply implementing the changes and announcing it after the fact. That's not change control, that's a free-for-all. Once I made only the most useful fields "required," the team started using the form and I was able to rein in the execution. The funny part about that whole story is that I never got dinged in a compliance audit for "improperly" filled out change request forms. So while you may be required to use a specific form or tool, make sure that it serves your needs before you put too much energy into using it.

Now let's talk about where you go to find out about any specific forms or tools you're expected to use. Your first stop should be your organization's PMO. These folks are generally happy to help you get started and can provide the templates and work instructions you need. They will also set you up with any tools of record you need to use. Wait! What do I mean by "tools of record"? Let me explain: here I'm talking about the web tools you will be required to enter your project data into. These tools are frequently used to make project execution progress visible to the organization's management chain and to provide a mechanism to track compliance to project management processes you are required to follow. You may be asked to upload/track data like resource spending (hours billed, for instance), project specific metrics such as Earned Value Metrics (EVM), and schedule performance to plan data, budget consumption, etc. Since your PMO really cares about these systems and this data, they take pains to document this stuff, so you probably only need to tap into the right person to get started. If your organization does not have a PMO, then you will probably need to ping a more experienced PM in the group to see what they consider to be required processes or forms. Chances are in that scenario there are very few "required" items you need to incorporate, since there's no PMO to enforce compliance, but there may be some tools you need to use for budgeting and resource-tracking purposes, so do a little digging and set those things up now.

Finally, there are a few more things you need to search out while you're looking for any other project management requirements your team needs to fulfill, and these are the compliance deliverables: things like regulatory, safety, and legal reviews and approvals. Sadly, it's not uncommon for some of these items to get lost in the shuffling requirements, as if a magician pocketed a marked card from the deck. As the PM you need to be on the lookout for things like safety reviews that require approval from a designated review board. These boards often have specific checklists or requirements that your project output will have to satisfy, so you need to make sure that this sort of compliance work is comprehended in the project requirements and in your project schedule. Let me tell you that it's mighty unpleasant to do a last-minute scramble to get Legal to sign off on some marketing collateral because no one remembered that you can't publish it until Legal has approved it. One note of caution here: you need to be cognizant of what types of compliance requirements are common for your particular industry. Don't rely on your subject matter experts and project team to know this stuff, because they may simply be working from the *"this is how we've always done it"* mindset. Yes, I've had senior technical people tell me that a safety review wasn't needed despite the fact that we were shipping a physical product to an external customer, and I've had managers tell me that we didn't need Marketing to approve the branding we were designing into a silkscreen for a control box. This is definitely one area where it pays to do your homework and make sure that your project plan comprehends any compliance requirements up front. Finally, another good resource for identifying these kinds of requirements are the experienced PMs in your organization, so go talk to them to make sure that your team isn't missing any major requirements that might be on the periphery of your project deliverables.

Develop the Schedule—The First Draft

Once you have the requirements identified, then you're ready to start building the project schedule. We are actually going to tackle the project schedule in two steps; we will make a first pass now, and then we will optimize it at the end of this chapter. Therefore, it's not necessary to have 100% of your requirements defined at this point in time, but you do need a solid 80% to proceed. Many junior project managers find this to be the hardest project artifact to create, but if you follow the systematic process I'll outline here, then you'll see that what appears at first glance to be a monster task is really a set of completely doable subtasks. Here we will build the draft of the schedule using a three-step process. The good news is that each of these steps is simple to master and once strung together produce a pretty decent schedule, even before we optimize it. The first step is to build what we PM practitioners call a Work Breakdown Structure, a.k.a. the WBS. The second step is to string the tasks identified in the WBS into a logical flow which we call the Network Diagram, and after that we transfer the flow of tasks into whichever scheduling software application we like to generate our project schedule. (Figure 3-1)

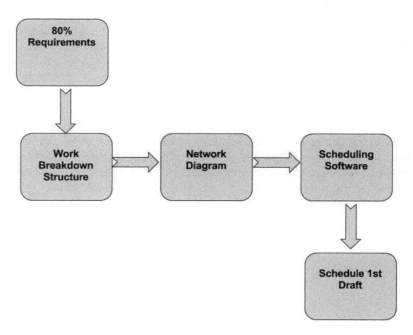

Figure 3-1. Draft schedule development flow

Develop the WBS

The good news is that the WBS is the easiest project artifact you and your team will produce, and you can usually knock it out in a couple of hours. Here's the deal; you and your team will start with the identified project deliverables and devolve them into actual work tasks, building a WBS in the process. To build the WBS, you start with the primary deliverables of your project. Then, for each of these primary deliverables you identify the sub-deliverables. For each sub-deliverable, you break them down further until you get to tasks. (Figure 3-2) Let me give you an example of what I'm talking about here. You start with a major project deliverable: something like, say, the Product Documentation. That documentation has sub-deliverables, one of which is going to be the User's Manual as an example. You can break the User's Manual into subparts such as the Wiring Diagram and the Assembly Instructions. At some point, your sub-deliverables become tasks such "Create the Wiring Diagram" and "Verify the Wiring Diagram." You and your team break down each primary deliverable until you get down to the task level you want to track in the schedule. For each task, capture who will perform the task and how long they think it will take to complete. You may need to break some tasks down to a more manageable size depending on the work. For instance, if the task is something like "Build the control box," you might need to break that down further if it's an especially long or complicated piece of work. Large chunks of work like this are called work packages in PM-speak and are usually associated with a schedule milestone, but more on that later. Once you've broken down a major deliverable into its specific work tasks, you move to the next one and lather, rinse, repeat until you and your team have broken down all of the work to execute the project. When you think you're done, do a gut check and ask the team this: "*Okay, folks, does it look like we've captured all of the work we need to do to execute this project?*" The point here is twofold; one, you want to leverage the collective experience of the team to verify that the breakdown is comprehensive, and two, you want to build buy-in with your teammates for the final schedule.

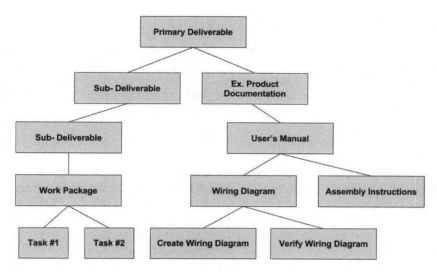

Figure 3-2. WBS example

This process appears to be pretty simple and straightforward to execute, doesn't it? Well, that's because it is! Yes, this is a perfect example of what I've been talking about. The hardest part about creating a WBS is first convincing the team that they need to do it and second refereeing the inevitable discussion of who owns each task. Over the years, I've found that it's a pretty easy sell to convince the team to do this exercise, and the refereeing is usually limited to a handful of tasks. If I'm working with a co-located team or a team that's able to gather physically to do the project planning, then I go old school and do this exercise on a big blank wall with a pile of sticky notes and markers. The team lays out the WBS similar to the way you would lay out an organizational chart, in a hierarchical manner. You could also just clump the tasks together by deliverable at this stage because it doesn't really matter. The important thing is to systematically break down the work to ensure that the team captures all of the work packages and tasks. If I'm working with a virtual team, then we will use mind-mapping software, a spreadsheet, or a collaboration tool that allows us to capture the breakdown. At this point you're not worried about the order in which the tasks will be performed; that comes next when you build the Network Diagram.

Develop the Network Diagram

Now that you've got all of the work you need to do to execute the project identified, it's time to start laying it out in a logical manner on a timeline. To create the Network Diagram, you basically line up the tasks and work packages in the order in which they will be performed, that is, the workflow. Start by drawing a timeline, starting with the milestone "Project Start" and ending with "Project Complete." Add in any major dates or milestones the team will need to anchor the workflow to, such as customer commitments, interim deliverables, key project milestones such as gate reviews, etc. If you don't have an exact date for these milestones, that's okay, just put them where you think they make the most sense for now. These are just stakes in the ground to anchor the diagram, and the actual dates for them will be adjusted later. You only need two, Start and Complete, to get started, but it's often helpful to add a few intermediate stakes into your timeline to help the team lay out the workflow. Next, move the tasks and work packages from the WBS to the timeline where they make the most sense. The goal here is to nail down the best workflow for the project, so expect to move the tasks around until you get a flow that makes the most sense. Step back from the diagram and see if there are places where more work can be done in parallel and be sure that each task has whatever deliverable it needs to start work lined up appropriately. Next, optimize the flow. As a team, walk through the flow, adjusting and tweaking it as needed until everyone is in agreement. Now draw connecting lines between the tasks to illustrate the workflow, carefully connecting all of the tasks to each other. Last, number each task sequentially along the workflow. Boom! That's your Network Diagram completed!

For teams that are physically able to do this planning work together, you have each team member move the sticky notes they own to the appropriate place on the timeline. The "timeline" consists of a long strip of paper, such as butcher paper, taped to the wall. After all of the sticky notes are transferred to the timeline, the team walks through the flow, moving the sticky notes around until the flow is optimized. Linkages are drawn and each note gets an index number. For teams that are doing this work virtually, it's especially helpful to use a software application that allows the team to drag and drop objects representing the tasks around to build a virtual project timeline "wall." Mind-mapping software is particularly good for this type of work. It should be noted that this type of planning is especially hard to do virtually, so if you've got a virtual team, then you really need to think hard about the best way to execute the WBS and the Network Diagram. Often, virtual teams do a lot of pre-work independently, coming together only at the end to walk the workflow and finalize the Network Diagram.

Building the Draft Schedule

Let's recap, shall we? At this point in the schedule development process, you should know:

1. All of the deliverables for the project

2. All of the work packages and tasks needed to produce the deliverables and execute the project

3. The owner for each task

4. How long each task is estimated to take

5. The predecessors and successors for each task, that is, the workflow

6. The Task ID number

If you are missing any one of these pieces of data, then stop right here and go find it. Do not proceed to building a schedule without this core knowledge base. The next step in the schedule development process is to use this core data set to build a project schedule using some type of scheduling application. Every cryin', cussin', spittin' fit I've ever had over a scheduling application was due to the fact that I didn't start with this core set of data. This is definitely a case of "garbage in, garbage out," so take my advice and don't start until you have the full data set.

The choice of scheduling application is up to you and is dependent on the project methodology you are using. These applications vary quite a bit, so I'm not going into the specifics for any particular one; instead, I'm going to walk you through a high-level process. If you a new user of this type of software, then do yourself a favor and take some basic user training before you start. Your first step is to set up the project parameters such as the type of calendar to use, the start date, how frequently file saves happen, units of measure for time (e.g., weeks, hours, minutes): basically, the typical configuration settings you tweak for other applications. Next, load in any non-working days such as company holidays for the expected duration of your project; extend your schedule end date a few weeks in case the project runs long.

Now you're ready to start entering specific tasks and milestones. You're going to use "milestones" to differentiate work packages, to mark significant dates, to structure your status reports around, and to measure progress against. For the most part you enter these babies into your scheduling software just like you would a task, and there's usually a field you toggle to assign these items a zero duration. So always start with your "Project Start" milestone as your first line item entered into the schedule. At this point you have a choice to make: do you want to enter each project task sequentially from the Network Diagram using the Task ID or do you want to group tasks by ownership, and by that I mean group all of the tasks for each functional area together? There's no right or wrong answer here; it's purely a matter of personal preference. It's easier to enter the tasks sequentially, because you can just leverage your Network Diagram Task ID numbers and enter each task in order of appearance in the flow. However, this does make it harder to view all of the tasks for a specific functional area. I prefer to lay out tasks sequentially by functional area so that I can "see" all of the work for each sub-team at one time; this, however, makes the data entry harder. Most types of scheduling software allow you to set up flags and filters to handle however you'd like to see the data so again, there's really no wrong way to go here. If you're a first-timer, then do yourself a favor and just lay out the tasks in the order they appear on the Network Diagram. Why borrow trouble, right? As you proceed through the Execution Phase, the tasks will be ordered in your schedule to align with the workflow and it's much easier to follow along. As you enter tasks, be sure that you're entering in the owner, work estimate, predecessors, and successors for each task as you go. *Do not enter specific start and finish dates.* The goal here is to make the software do the work of figuring out those dates so only enter start/finish dates for milestones representing incoming deliverables. The best practice is to manually enter start/finish dates for as few tasks or milestones as possible because these dates artificially constrain the scheduling software and that's not really what you want to happen. Insert milestones as needed to help you keep track of the execution progress. I separate major work packages with start/end milestones; for example, I'll use a "Development Start" milestone and a "Development Complete" milestone so that I can report out on the status of that "Development Complete" milestone throughout the life of the project. Use milestones liberally to help group the work packages; just be sure that each milestone is set to zero duration and that it has at least one predecessor and one successor.

Once you've entered all of your tasks and finished typing the "Project Complete" milestone, jump up and do a quick happy dance! You've just completed 75% of the work to create your project schedule! Notice that the hardest part of this whole process so far has been wrestling with the scheduling software? If you took my advice and made sure that you had a complete core set of data to start with, then I bet that you were surprised at how painless using that scheduling software was as well. Obviously, just how "easy" that process was is dependent on how much effort you put into learning how to use the scheduling software, so make the time to do that training.

Okay, sit back down and let's do a little housekeeping before we call that draft schedule done. First, double-check that each task is linked into a continuous chain or flow. In a perfect schedule, the only two line items that won't have a predecessor and a successor are the "Project Start" and "Project Complete" milestones. Do your best to achieve perfection. Next, look for any tasks with dates you've manually entered: there should only be a few of them, and they all should be milestones representing external deliverables into the project workflow. Look at the critical path or chain depending on the software you are using.

Does it make sense? Are the tasks you were expecting to be there on it? If not, figure out where the logic is breaking down and fix it. Now verify that each task has a resource assigned to it. I assign myself, as the PM, ownership of all of the milestones on the schedule. Finally get with your subject matter experts and do a sanity check. Ask things like *"does it make sense that the code development will take 4 months?"* and *"is it reasonable that the marketing collateral will take 2 weeks to complete?"* Once you're satisfied that all of these troubleshooting areas have been resolved, then it's time to call this draft schedule done!

A WORD ABOUT DATES AND WHY THEY DON'T MATTER AT THIS STAGE OF THE GAME

Okay, right about now you're probably freaking out because the Project Complete date is not the date you were told to hit, is it? Relax, this is exactly what should be happening at this stage of the planning. In fact, it's very rare for the schedule to line up exactly with the target date the team was given during scoping. So what's going on and why do I think these dates don't matter that much at this stage of the game? Until you've optimized the project schedule, any dates that are generated so far are speculative at best. There are too many factors in play right now to lock in on a specific date and believe that it's set in stone. For instance, while the team is building the Network Diagram, they may come to the realization that they can't hit the desired project delivery date. However, this layout doesn't take into account holidays, individual vacations, the intricacies of coordinating highly interdependent work packages, the parallel nature of some of the work, etc., so it's not really surprising that those dates are not accurate. Your draft schedule is just that, a draft that we will optimize after we've done some more planning. So relax, you're doing it right! Care should be taken to manage your teammates' and stakeholders' expectations at this point in time. Remind them that these dates are early indicators and that all of the factors that contribute to the finished schedule aren't baked in yet. In fact, I usually take precautions to hide the dates as they appear in the scheduling software while the team is validating the schedule logic to avoid mass paranoia and "sky is falling" soliloquies.

Build the Release Readiness Checklist

Once the deliverables are solid, you need to think a bit about the release process and build a Release Readiness Checklist. This step must be done before you optimize your schedule, but it can be done at any point in the planning workflow. I most frequently find myself doing it after I've completed the draft schedule. The Release Readiness Checklist is pretty much what it sounds like: a checklist of items that must be completed before the project deliverable can be released. The items on this checklist are what I consider "due diligence" items, that is, items that must be done to ensure that the end product is safe and secure, meets all necessary compliance requirements, and has been created using industry best practices. You need to find, or create, this checklist now because part of the schedule optimization we will discuss later includes making sure that the items on this checklist have corresponding work packages in the project schedule. In more mature project management organizations, these checklists already exist and all you need to do is use them. However, if there's no such creature in your world, then you will need to create it, so let's talk about how you go about constructing one.

Creating the Release Readiness Checklist is another one of those straightforward PM tasks that if taken on independently is easy to knock out. I prefer to use a spreadsheet, but really you can use whatever software you like for this task. Structurally, you want to have a list of items, a spot (a.k.a. a checkbox) to indicate whether or not the task was completed, a place for notes for each item, and some contextual notes on the project such as the project name, revisions, scope of work considered, etc. Write each item as a question, something like this: *"Are all personally identifiable data encrypted in storage and in transit?"* As to what exactly needs to be on the checklist, start with best practices, which are things like design reviews, validation of the design, defect closure and management, compliance to corporate standards such as branding or privacy, etc. Next, consider safety and what needs to be done to attain compliance approval for the project deliverables. Consider items such as customer acceptance criteria and other quantifiable metrics the project objective may call out. Finally, consider the release process itself: Are there any formal approvals that need to be obtained? Change requests that need to be submitted? If so, then there needs to be a corresponding item on the checklist. Don't forget to include logistical items for the release planning such as scheduling and availability of resources. The final checklist for your specific project probably won't be longer than 20–30 items depending on the scope of your project. Remember these are the absolute "must-do" items that the team needs to accomplish, and anything that garners a "No" on the checklist is a showstopper and should get serious scrutiny before deciding whether or not to release the project. After you have your checklist complete, shop it around to your teammates and key stakeholders to make sure that you haven't missed anything. Once you've secured agreement on the checklist items, you can put it away for now. We'll refer to it when we optimize the schedule, but we will actually use it later for the release planning in Chapter 4.

Develop the Risk Management Plan

We come now to the most frequently skipped project management process out there, developing the risk management plan. Da-duh ... Da-duh ... Da-duh ... can you hear the *Jaws* music yet? Okay, it's actually not that bad, and I think most PMs, senior ones included, struggle with developing the risk management plan because while the actual mechanics of risk management are simple to learn, it requires the PM to motivate, negotiate, referee, and lead their team to complete the risk planning, and that's a whole other kettle of fish. Once again, we see that the mechanics are simple, but the soft skills needed to be successful make this work harder than it has to be. So, like the broken record I've become, let me say it again: master the mechanics so that you will have more time and energy to deal with the interpersonal challenges of project management.

The biggest hurdle to implementing risk management is the perception that the whole thing is a complicated, bureaucratic hot mess that mostly wastes the team's time. To overcome this perception, I'm going to help you streamline the process and craft it into something you and your project team can actually use. In case you're tempted to skip this process, let me just say that I believe the risk management process alone is the single best tool a PM has for reducing the need for frantic firefighting during the Execution Phase. You see we are going to plan for those potential fires and tee up responses so that when the embers of a potential forest fire spark up, the team is ready with a plan that effectively douses that spark with good solid execution.

Risk planning is, like so much of project planning, a three-step process: first we collect the risks, then we rank 'em, and finally we develop plans to deal with the top risks. To collect potential project risks, facilitate a brainstorming session with your project team. The idea here is to identify as many risks as possible, so don't get hung up on how reasonable each suggestion is. To get a rich set of risks, pose future-thinking questions like *"We just released this project deliverable and no one is buying it. What happened?"* and *"The product is wildly successful so now manufacturing can't keep up with the demand. What did we miss?"* Like all brainstorming sessions, the team eventually winds down, so move to the next step, which is ranking the identified risks. To rank the risks you need two scales: one for the impact of the risk if it were to occur and one for the probability that the risk will occur. These scales are completely arbitrary, so just make a balanced one up; be sure to use an even number of scaling options, such as a scale of 1–4. If you were to choose a scale of 1–9, for instance, what you will find is that some of your team won't want to choose sides and will take the middle ground of a 5. If enough people choose a 5, then you end up with every risk being rated as equally likely/impactful, which doesn't help, so construct your scale with an even number of options. It's quite common for some of your teammates to offer up wildly improbable risks and advocate for them passionately. This is not a big deal and you can defuse a potentially ratholed discussion by simply agreeing to add their pet risk to the list. During the rating process, many of these risks will drop out due to the fact that the likelihood of occurrence is so low. Therefore, save yourself the headache and don't make an issue of their crazy talk. For most small to midsized projects, a team can identify and rate potential risks in an hour or two. In the case of large projects, it's likely that there already exists a required tool of record for recording and tracking project risks. In these cases risk identification and rating can take a while to complete. (Figure 3-3)

Figure 3-3. Risk planning flow diagram

Once all of the identified risks have been rated for probability of occurrence and impact, it's time to rank them. The risk ranking is a simple formula; the rank is equal to the occurrence rating multiplied by the impact rating. If you order your risks by ranking, then you should see the most urgent risks to address at the top of the list. By the way, this list with each risk listed including the ratings and rankings is referred to as the risk register. Cool, huh? You're now throwing down PMI-blessed terminology! The next step is to apply a little common sense. As a team, review the list of ranked risks and determine which of the top contenders the team can actually affect. It's pointless and frustrating to argue around a risk the team cannot address. For example, I commonly hear the risk *"resources may be pulled off the project"*; well, sure, that can happen, but at the risk-planning point in the project, there are no plans to do that, so why waste time arguing about it? If there's a likelihood that a specific resource will be pulled away, then that's something we can plan around, but a nebulous risk that cannot be predicted or affected is not something the team can plan for. We call that an *unknown unknown* in PM-speak. As a team, identify the top three to five risks you want to address. Why only three to five risks? Well, in my experience, that's the most reasonable number of risks a team can tackle at one time without suffering a hit on their productivity. If your team has the bandwidth and you've already addressed the top risks, you can always add more into the risk management plan as time allows, but for now just focus on those top three to five risks.

So far, so good right? You've now got a list of three to five risks you need to develop plans around, so let's talk about risk planning now. The trick to risk management planning is realizing that there are only five ways to deal with a potential risk, and they are as follows:

- **Mitigation—take specific actions to prevent or lessen the impact of the risk occurring**

- **Contingency—take specific actions to reduce the impact of the risk once it has occurred**

- **Transference—take specific actions to transfer the risk to another entity**

- **Acceptance—do nothing and accept the impact if the risk occurs**

- **Avoidance—take specific actions to avoid the likelihood and impact of the risk occurring**

That's it! Once you can wrap your head around the fact that you only have these five options, risk management plans get a whole lot easier to develop. Walk through these five options for each risk and determine which actions the team will take (or not take) in anticipation of the risk occurring and once it does in fact occur. The actions the team decides to take here need to be incorporated back into your schedule as specific tasks. By doing this, you take away much of the bureaucracy commonly associated with the risk management process. These tasks are now tracked as part of the regular project work and are monitored and controlled as such. We'll talk more about this later, but for now, just understand that it's important that you translate your risk management plans into specific tasks embedded into the project schedule. You will probably select more than one option for the really important risks to address and you will be choosing to accept all of the risks you do not address. This is okay, and it's perfectly legitimate to state that acceptance up front. One final note here on how to record your risk management plans. Since I integrate the tasks associated with managing each risk the team takes on into the project schedule, the weekly team meeting minutes are where any updates to the risk plans are documented. However, many organizations require the PM to log risks and track risks into a formal risk register. These are frequently separate web tools or documents that the PM is expected to maintain. Maintaining a separate risk register is a duplication of effort if you've incorporated your risk plans into your schedule, so this is one area where I put as little effort as possible into compliance.

Optimize the Schedule

Okay, we're almost done with planning your first project; in fact, we're so close you can practically smell the baseline! The only thing left to do is optimize the schedule, so let's get to it. The first thing you need to do is verify that all project work is represented in the schedule. If you will recall, you might have built the WBS with only 80% of the project requirements documented, so it's time to double back and make sure that all of the documented requirements have associated tasks in the schedule. Ensure that all of the items on the Release Readiness Checklist have representative tasks in the schedule. Do the same thing for your risk management plans. It's not uncommon for some of the work packages or risk plans to have some ambiguity about them. For instance, the technical lead is waiting for final feedback from the security architect, which may result in a new requirement. For these ambiguous tasks, you need to enter a placeholder task into the schedule and give it a conservative work estimate. These placeholder tasks are really schedule buffers, and we'll talk more about them later. The key thing here is to mitigate the ambiguity by adding these buffers. In the case of risk management, you may not know if the risk has occurred, so you need to add tasks to test whether or not the risk is active. These are simple tasks such as *"Check the weather forecast before committing to the foundation pour."* In that example, if bad weather is expected and pouring the foundation will be delayed, the next task in the workflow is a weather buffer task which is activated. If there's no expected delay, that task can be inactivated or marked as completed with zero duration. Once you're sure that you've captured all of the known work, it's time to move to the next step.

After verifying that all of the work is represented, you need to make sure that all holidays and any non-working days are captured in the scheduling tool. Be sure to include team members' planned vacations, training, etc. It can be a hassle to get your teammates to provide their vacation plans, especially if you're asking in February and they haven't even started thinking about their summer vacation. In those cases, put in a placeholder for any vacation or training time they might have that will last longer than a few days. (FYI, these non-working days are tracked in the calendar function of your scheduling application and are not specific tasks in the schedule.) It's prudent to plan for those times when your team members will not be working on your project up front to avoid having those same folks working overtime to catch up on the project work once they return. If the project will span the end-of-year holidays such as Thanksgiving, Christmas, and New Year's, I block the full week for each holiday as non-working days. I do the same thing for Chinese New Year as needed. This provides a little extra buffer for the schedule and accounts for the fact that much of the team will be taking time off.

Speaking of buffers, it's now time to add some more. For each of the major work packages, add a buffer task to the schedule in anticipation of those unknown unknowns we talked about earlier. Place these buffer tasks right before the completion milestone and make it a predecessor for the next task in the workflow. Don't worry about how much work to assign to each buffer yet; simply add them into the schedule between major work packages or milestones. I typically buffer the development work, the validation work, and a catchall buffer right before the project release milestone. To figure out how much buffer you need, look at the total estimated work and calculate a percentage of the total to distribute across the project timeline. For projects where I feel we have high confidence in the requirements and low to moderate risk, I will typically use a buffer of 15%; for projects where there are still a lot of unknowns and the risk is higher I will use 25%. Obviously, how much buffer you use is a matter of experience so if you're not sure just start with 20%. This buffered schedule is your "worst-case" scenario, which means that even if things go slightly sideways and the team encounters some obstacles you didn't plan for, you can still hit the buffered release commitment. As long as nothing unexpected and grossly impactful happens, your team can deliver to this schedule; it's your "high-confidence" commit. The flip side is also true; even if things go swimmingly, the likelihood of the team delivering the project much earlier than this buffered date is low. You and your management chain may not like this date, but it is the most likely date the team can deliver to unless specific actions are taken to pull in the schedule.

MORE ON BUFFERING A SCHEDULE

Yes, a buffered schedule yields a high-confidence commitment to deliver, but is that realistic? Many organizations view schedule buffers as evil padding and heavily scrutinize any project schedule in an attempt to stomp out buffers. This is extremely short-sighted in my opinion, because you are then planning for nothing to go wrong, for the sun to always shine, and the design to always work. That's just not realistic, is it? Instead, I look at buffers as part of responsible project planning. A well-buffered schedule dramatically increases the predictability of delivering the project on time, and isn't that the point of planning in the first place? High predictability of project execution allows an organization to better utilize resources and coordinate work across programs. Further, a buffered schedule ensures that the team isn't burnt out at the end because delays and unexpected risks were planned for.

Pull In the Release Date (if Needed)

At this point, you're probably caught between a rock (the stakeholder's expectations) and a hard place (the high-confidence schedule), and you need to figure out what to do next. It's important to realize a key point here. The stakeholder expectations are primarily based on business needs and possibly a commitment to a customer. They are not based on the actual work needed to produce the project deliverables. The high-confidence schedule is solidly grounded in the actual work content and may not meet that business need. It's now time to optimize the schedule to see if it's possible to bridge the gap between the stakeholders' expectations and reality.

Your first step when pulling in a schedule is to look for ways to optimize the workflow. This is the low-hanging fruit. Identify work that can be done in parallel and reorder the workflow to shorten the overall project duration. Look for specific tasks that can start earlier with a partial predecessor deliverable. Any work you can move off of the critical path will shorten the overall project duration, so carefully scrutinize those tasks and see if there are opportunities to reorder the work. Once you've done all of the workflow optimization you can, baseline your schedule and make a copy. You will use this copy to do "what-if" scenario modeling next.

In Chapter 2 we discussed the Triple Constraint and the fact that you must balance the project's schedule, scope, and resources. If you recall, there really are only two ways to pull in your project schedule—either reduce the scope of work or add more resources—so let's dig a little deeper into what that looks like.

Reducing the scope of work is often the most realistic way to pull in a schedule since resources don't grow on trees. As a team, carefully scrutinize the requirements and identify any that are considered "nice to haves" or that can be delayed. Consider using a phased approach to implementing requirements that will allow the team to deliver the most important functionality on time. Another completely viable, though unpopular, strategy is to reduce the quality of the project deliverable through reducing the amount of validation to be performed, so that again, the most important functionality can be delivered on time. Use that copy of the schedule you made to do "what-if" scenario modeling by cutting tasks from the schedule to understand the impact to the overall timeline. Be sure to keep track of the schedule impact each of these reduced-scope options generates.

Adding resources to the schedule is called *"crashing the schedule."* Cute name, huh? Who says project managers don't have a sense of humor? Often junior project managers go to their stakeholders with a generic ask for more resources: *"We need five more resources to be able to release this product by the end of October."* The problem here is that this ask is too vague and not actionable by the stakeholders. The trick to getting more resources is to identify specific work packages to apply them to, in order to accelerate the schedule. To do this, you take your "what-if" scenario modeling schedule and add resources to tasks on the critical path to see what the impact to the final date will be. By doing this modeling, you and your team can identify some strategic work packages where additional resources can have a meaningful impact. Now the ask looks something like this: *"If we can get an additional database analyst for the first two weeks of June, then we can pull the schedule in by three weeks."* Now, the stakeholder who can provide that resource knows exactly what you need and when you need it, and your stakeholder is more likely to act.

At this point, you should have your high-confidence schedule and several options for pulling it in, so now it's time to negotiate with your stakeholders. This negotiation is often contentious and difficult because the project manager hasn't done their homework. The job of the project manager here is to provide viable options to the decision-makers. We get paid whether we execute Plan A or Plan B, but it's our responsibility to provide the data to the decision-makers so that they can make informed decisions about additional resources or reduced scope. The careful planning you and your team have done so far has generated that data through the "what-if" scenario modeling, and while your stakeholders may huff and puff a bit, eventually they will face reality and make some decisions that allow you to lock in the plan and schedule. At this point, you can obtain stakeholder buy-off on the major project milestones, so update your baseline schedule with any changes based on these negotiations. Re-baseline the schedule and use these dates as your commitment to deliver. Last, send out a formal communication committing the project to these new dates.

That's it! You are finished planning your project! The Planning Phase is where most of the mechanics of project management happen, and it's all downhill from here with respect to artifacts you need to generate or specific PM processes you need to follow.

Checklist #2—The Planning Phase

The Planning Phase of the project is where the work really happens when it comes to project mechanics. We've covered a lot of ground here, so be sure to use this checklist to keep yourself on track. Just like Checklist #1, these items are arranged in chronological order but you may end up completing them in any order; the important thing is to do them all before proceeding to the next phase of the project.

Checklist #2—The Planning Phase

☐ Regular team meetings have been scheduled for the expected duration of the project

☐ The communication plan has been completed

☐ Project lifecycle model has been identified

☐ Project requirements are frozen and formal change control is now in effect

☐ Change Control Board has been established

☐ The Release Readiness Checklist has been developed

☐ The risk register has been developed and the top risks have active risk management plans identified

☐ All stakeholders agree to the project timeline milestones

☐ Schedule has been baselined

☐ The committed project schedule has been communicated to the organization

---

Congratulations! You've just exited the Planning Phase of your project! You've now completed the majority of the project management processes and produced the bulk of the artifacts you will need to manage the project. All that's left now is to put your planning into action in the Execution Phase, which comes next.

Executing Your First Project

a.k.a. The Execution Phase

By this point in time, you should have completed all of the items on Checklist #2; that is, you should have a solid project plan. In the Execution Phase of the project you will move from creating project management artifacts into using them. Here you will leverage the work you did to kick off the project and the stakeholder management plan to facilitate regular team meetings. You will use your project Change Control Board to participate in the program- or organization-level Change Control Board(s). You will utilize the project schedule to track work and gauge progress. Risks will be triggered, and those action plans you and your team developed to deal with potential risks will be activated. Finally, you will use all of the artifacts you've created to generate regular status updates and manage escalations. The bulk of the project work does happen in this phase; however, since you've taken care of business in the Planning Phase, Execution for the project manager is about using the tools you developed previously. At this point in time, you are probably feeling a little shell-shocked since the Planning Phase involved a lot of work. Don't worry; the mechanics of the job will be significantly easier going forward.

© Melanie McBride 2016
M. McBride, *Project Management Basics*, DOI 10.1007/978-1-4842-2086-3_4

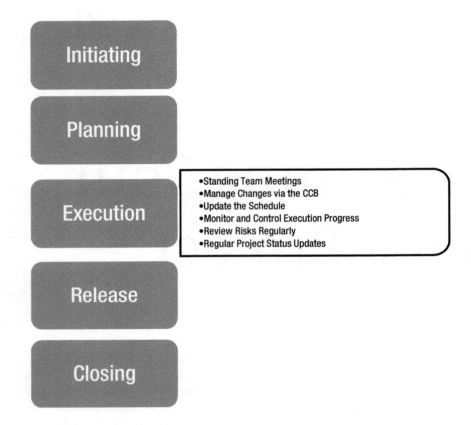

Initiating

Planning

Execution
- •Standing Team Meetings
- •Manage Changes via the CCB
- •Update the Schedule
- •Monitor and Control Execution Progress
- •Review Risks Regularly
- •Regular Project Status Updates

Release

Closing

Holding Regular Team Meetings

By the time you've exited the Planning Phase, you've already got a standing team meeting set up, however this is a great time to fine-tune your meeting dynamic. First, think about the content of this meeting, a.k.a. the agenda. It needs to be a balance of au courant topics and team updates. I suggest breaking your agenda up like this: 10% of the time for your project CCB, 60% for team updates, 20% to discuss the schedule, and the remaining 10% of the meeting to reviewing action items, next steps, help needed, and any open questions the team might have. The trick here is to devote enough time to the team updates but still address the business of managing the project, so let me break this down a bit further for you. That 10% devoted to the CCB is not always needed, so here's where you can fit in meatier topics the team needs to discuss on a periodic basis. Note that if the special topic is especially controversial or involved, you may need to adjust the meeting time to go longer. The individual team updates should constitute the bulk of the meeting time and discussion. It's a good idea to set expectations that each team member come prepared to discuss what they've accomplished, any help they need, what they plan to work on next, and any new developments in their domain. The goal is to get succinct updates from each team member and it may take some coaching and a bit of time for the team to get into this groove. I prefer to cover the schedule updates after the individual team updates because this serves as a recap of the update portion of the meeting. There are two goals here: one is to ensure that each team member understands what work they are accountable for and when it's due, and the second goal is to validate the schedule logic and ensure that it matches reality. The last bit of the agenda is dedicated to housekeeping, that is, updates on open action items that the team hasn't already discussed, reviewing any next steps the team has decided to take, and time for any questions the team may have that were not previously covered. I prefer to discuss these items at the end of the meeting because I've found that for the most part these open action items organically come up during the team updates and accompanying discussion. The time at the end of the agenda is mostly used to capture anything we missed talking about earlier and individual team members' out-of-office plans.

Now that you know what content the meeting will address, it's time to tweak the logistics. First, consider when your team meeting is happening. Do you have any team members who are always late or who regularly miss the team meeting? If so, then it's probably time to adjust the meeting timing. It should be during accepted working hours for each team member. But what exactly are "accepted working hours," anyway? We're talking 8 a.m. to 5 p.m., generally speaking. Sounds logical, right? Not so fast! There's more to this that first meets the eye. Many people have personal commitments or ugly commutes, so you should avoid the 8–9 a.m. window and the 4–5 p.m. window. Lunchtime meetings, or meetings that run over and extend into the lunch hour, are really bad ideas. Yes you can compel your team members to attend a meeting over their lunch hour, but they won't be happy about it and their level of engagement and willingness to take on more work will reflect their opinion of you co-opting their lunch hour. So this leaves us with these optimum meeting times: 9 a.m.–noon and 1 p.m.–4 p.m. It gets further complicated if your team resides in different time zones. See, I told you there was more to this than you thought. The best course of action is to find a time that works for everyone on the team in those optimum meeting timeframes. The second best option is to rotate the meeting times so that everyone shares the pain ... this month we meet at my 6 p.m. and next month we meet at your 7 a.m. This is a significant challenge for geo-dispersed teams, and it's one with no perfect solution in many cases. In fact, many teams prefer to pick one not-so-wonderful time and stick to it for the duration of the project rather than deal with rotating meetings. The best you can do is to check in with team members regularly and make adjustments as necessary.

Where you meet is as important as the agenda and when the meeting takes place. The first choice should always be to meet in person. Ironically, in our world of virtual meetings you may have to influence your team members to leave their desks and actually walk down to a conference room. It might have been a long time since they had regular, standing, in-person meetings! If you can't manage to meet in person, then use videoconferencing to improve communication. If you can't do in person or videoconferencing, then you're left with teleconferencing. Here it's important to have some way to "share your screen" so that everyone can see the same thing as the meeting progresses. This is where you want to take meeting minutes in real time while sharing that screen. Finally if all else fails, go old school and do the meeting with audio only. Remember, we all used to execute perfectly complex and complicated work with only telephones and e-mail; it can be done. If you're going the "audio-only" route, be sure to tell your teammates up front and let them know that they will need to follow along with collateral provided earlier and take their own notes. An "audio-only" meeting is not one they can effectively participate in from their car or in any venue without the ability to boot up their laptop and review the collateral. I always ask my teammates to take their own notes during audio-only meetings so that they stay engaged in the discussion. I still capture and distribute meeting minutes as part of my normal meeting facilitation duties.

Finally a word about meeting facilitation: do it! A poorly facilitated meeting is a waste of everyone's time and it degrades your ability to make progress as a team. Actively control the discussion and direct it to the agenda unless there's a very good reason to diverge. Ensure that an actual decision is made rather than the team just talking around an issue. This often requires the project manager to drive the discussion with statements like *"Okay, so what exactly are we going to do here?"* Be sure to pull in opinions and ideas from the entire team, especially those who appear to be on the fringes of the discussion. It's perfectly fine to sideline a topic for another discussion or forum if it's not central to the stated meeting agenda, and it's perfectly fine to add an adjacent topic into the agenda if it's germane to what the team is trying to achieve. Actively manage those meeting participants who tend to monopolize the discussion, and again, ensure that everyone gets to participate. At the end of the meeting, restate any decisions that the team has made and quickly review the action items to ensure that owners understand what they need to go do. Most importantly, end the meeting on time. If the discussion isn't finished, schedule a follow-up meeting. Meeting facilitation is a core project manager competency, and if you're not quite there yet, then you need to focus on building this skill quickly. A well-run meeting is like duct tape; it can fix darn near anything, so get comfortable facilitating meetings to improve your PM effectiveness.

Playing at the Program-Level CCB

In Chapter 3, we talked about streamlining your project change control process to remove bureaucracy and improve the team's ability to comprehend changes efficiently. Now it's time to consider how to manage changes within the realm of an overarching program or organization. Here you will leverage the project CCB infrastructure you've already built to feed into the higher-level

CCB. The first thing you need to do is figure out the change control process the program uses. There will likely be a specific change request form and an approval body, a.k.a. the Program CCB. Previously, I helped you sidestep the bureaucracy that often accompanies change control, but at some point your team will either need to implement a change that affects entities outside of the specific project's sphere of control or be asked to implement a change from those external entities. Now you're moving up from the farm team to the minor league of change control, so how do you do that?

If your project team is proposing the change, then you fill out the form and submit it for review. There are two keys to getting these proposed changes approved: supporting data and stakeholder management. Before even proposing the change, get that data. Your goal here is to quantify the change impact, so figure out how much it will cost or how long it will take and include that information within your change request. While you are pulling this data together, and before submitting the request, discuss this possible change with affected stakeholders. Remember those folks you identified in Planning? Those folks! Your goal is to get buy-in for the change before it's presented to the program CCB. Yes, this takes some time, and you could be doing something else, but here's the catch: if you submit a half-baked change request, then chances are you will be rejected and you'll need to revamp the request to try again. It takes longer to go through the "lather-rinse-repeat" cycle than it does to talk to the stakeholders before the CCB meeting. Plus, these change requests are great excuses to have a synch-up session with your major stakeholders; that is, they can be the stated purpose of a one-on-one meeting that you can then leverage to check in with those stakeholders to gauge how satisfied they are with your team's performance to date. In short, you kill two birds with one change request stone; you expedite the approval of your change request and you improve your relationship with key stakeholders. If you do your homework and grease the skids with your stakeholders, then the actual review of the request in the approval body is merely a rubber stamp and your change request is quickly approved. If you fail to address these two key success factors, then the approval body review of your change request will be frustrating and drawn-out, so just be prepared and avoid the headache.

You need a different strategy for those times when another group brings a change request to the program CCB. In a perfect world, the change submitter would have talked to you before submitting the request to understand the impact on your project team and your specific concerns. You don't work in a perfect world and you probably weren't consulted ahead of time. It's not uncommon for a proposed changed to be presented as a "must-do" change, and you may get some significant pressure to agree to execute it. Resist the temptation to give in without doing due diligence. Here's where you offer to *take this back to my team and understand the impact."* Your objective is to agree to assess the proposed change and bring back impact and options. You should never agree to a change, especially a major change, without understanding the potential impact. At this point, the change request will either be on hold or conditionally approved pending your impact analysis. Your next step is to meet with your team to discuss what it will take to implement this proposed change. Leverage your project schedule to do some "what-if" modeling just like you did when you optimized the schedule at the end of Planning. But don't stop there! Now see if you and your team can come up with some alternative options and model those as well. Once you've done this analysis, you're ready to go back to the program CCB with an impact and some options. In my experience, having solid supporting data blunts the peer pressure to simply approve the change request and figure out how to execute it later. By providing this supporting data, you enable the decision-maker(s) to make a data-based decision about how they want to proceed. Sure, you still may need to execute the change request, but by doing that analysis, your team has already figured out what work they need to do, and it's fairly easy to integrate the change into the project schedule.

A COMMON CHANGE CONTROL DILEMMA

While this book is not focused on the soft skills needed to lead projects, there's one "soft skills" challenge that seems to crop up all the time, and it's directly related to controlling changes. You see, it's quite likely that after you and your team have met to hash out that impact to the project for a proposed change, your teammates will go off and start executing the change before it's officially approved. You also see this at the project level, where a teammate is sure that the change must be implemented, so they just do it and submit the change request after the fact. In fact, it's very common, especially in high-performing teams, for the team to begin work on the change request before it's officially approved. Is that a bad thing? Possibly, since there's some chance that the change request will get denied. If that happens, then all of the work done to implement the change pre-CCB approval will need to be backed out. The flip side is also true, in that the change request could be approved and now your team is ahead of schedule for executing that change pre-approval. So what's a PM to do? Do you browbeat your team into stopping work on the change request before it's approved? To be honest, there's no "right" answer here and you have to go with your instincts and decide how likely the CCB is to approve the change. In general, I let my teams run with the implementation of the change while making it clear that there's still a possibility that the change will be denied and we will have to back out the change. If I've got a pretty strong feeling that the change will not be approved or will be approved with significant changes to the implementation, then I share that knowledge with the team to influence them to hold off on further changes. In either scenario, I make it clear that if we have to back out of the changes due to a denied change request, then we must do that without impacting the schedule. For the most part, this gamble to implement before approval pays off, but every once in a while it doesn't. It's your call as to how you want to proceed; just be very clear with your team about whether they should start, stop, or continue to implement the change before the CCB approval is obtained.

Iterate Schedule Updates

In the Planning Phase, you built a solid schedule, so now, during the Execution Phase, you need to keep it updated. Depending on the pace of work for your project, you will need to update your schedule on a regular cadence. In many cases weekly updates are the way to go. There are two categories of updates you will need to incorporate: progress against the planned work and additional, unplanned work. However you update your schedule, it is imperative that it model the project reality as closely as possible. Therefore, if you determine during your weekly team meeting that the database analyst is working on a major task that's not in the schedule, then you need to incorporate it into the existing workflow. You may not like what that does to the projected completion date, but there's no benefit to ignoring the fact that that work has to be done. Ignoring this extra work and its potential impact on the completion date is disingenuous and irresponsible. Your job is to monitor the project's progress and manage the execution, which you can't do if you don't understand what is really going on.

■ **Caution**   It is imperative that the schedule model the project reality as closely as possible.

The first category of updates is the progress of the planned work. In PM-speak you will hear this referred to as "Progress Against Schedule" (PAS), and we will talk more about that later when we get to the metrics discussion. Basically, this is where you update each task in the schedule based on the work updates your team provides. Your first choice to capture these updates should always be an automated system. The predominant schedule management software packages have advanced features that allow individuals to submit schedule updates via a web tool and cloud solution: the Microsoft Project Server solution is one example. Unfortunately, these advanced features come with a steep IT overhead, so you may not have access to them. The next-best option is to meet individually with each team member to discuss their work and capture their progress for all of the tasks they own. Note that this is often impractical due to the size of the project team and the team members' time constraints. So this leaves you with Door Number 3: capturing updates in your weekly team meeting. The wrong way to do this is to drag the entire team through a grueling step-by-step inspection of each task on the schedule. This is mind-numbingly boring for the team and unproductive in general, so stay away from this option. The better way to collect task updates in the meeting is to guide the discussion during the team updates to the major work that's going on. Ask things like *"So how's that wiring diagram coming along? Do you think you'll be done this week or is it going to push into next week?"* In this scenario, you should be sharing the project schedule so that everyone on the team can "see" it as they provide updates or as you walk through the schedule during the meeting.

Note that you will need to schedule in some time on your calendar to review the task-in-progress before the meeting so that you are ready to ask those sorts of questions. In short, collect the info you need to update the schedule organically through actual discussion rather than putting each team member on the spot while the others sit around twiddling their thumbs. If you chose to use mind-mapping software to develop your schedule, it's easy to facilitate this type of discussion. The main objective here is to avoid grilling your teammates like sausages at a convenience store food service area. Finally, the absolute worst way to collect progress updates it to set up a separate file that your team needs to update each week. Here you must monitor who has provided updates and transfer those updates to the actual project schedule. Why is this the worst way to do this job? Because your teammates will sporadically forget to update their tasks and you'll have to go nag them to provide their updates. You are now also stuck with a separate file you need to keep in synch with the schedule. Trust me, this is a huge time sink, so avoid collecting your schedule updates this way.

That's the "how" to capture the progress updates; now let's talk about what information you're actually going to grab and use to update your schedule. Depending on the organization you work in, this can be completely up to you as the project manager or it can be mandated that you collect the actual hours spent on executing your particular project. The good news is that if the organization cares and actually uses actual hours, then systems are in place to capture that information, which in turn makes the job of updating the schedule easier. It's actually harder to determine what you need if there's no expectations or mandates you have to follow. If you have access to those advanced software package features, then the best way to go is to collect the actual hours applied to each task. This information is extremely valuable for estimating future projects and managing an organization's project pipeline. However, as a junior project manager you may only use this information to monitor the project costs and some execution metrics. The difficulty with collecting actual hours, however, is that it's extremely challenging for your teammates to track these hours unless there's some infrastructure in place for them to do so. In summary, if the organization has the tools to track actual hours, then go for it; if they don't have that infrastructure then there's a simpler way to go. The simpler way to go is to forego the accuracy of actual hours in favor of the "good-enough" accuracy of percentage of the work complete. Here's how it works: if a task is started give it a 25% completion rating; once the task owner indicates that the work is "halfway done," the task gets updated to 50%; and of course, when the task is complete it's set to 100% complete. That's it; each task gets four options for percentage complete: 0%, 25%, 50%, and 100%. The problem with this method is that it's entirely subjective and based on the task owner's estimate of how much work remains to be done. Percentage complete is also a reactive metric as it does not forecast when the task will be done; it's simply a snapshot in time, and projecting out a completion date with percentage complete metrics assumes that the future work will continue at the same pace. In fact, many project management experts will tell you that using percentage complete to track progress against the schedule is weak and inaccurate. They are right, of course, but here's the thing: it's good enough for what you're doing, so relax and use percentage complete if that's what's reasonable for your project environment. Remember, the goal is to use the schedule to monitor the project execution, and if percentage complete gets the job done, then use it.

The second category of schedule updates is tracking any unplanned work that gets added into the workflow throughout execution. As change requests are approved and unexpected work gets added, it's important to incorporate those tasks into the schedule so that you have a realistic projected completion date. Each time some of this unplanned work pops up, determine if it can be absorbed without impacting the current project timeline. If it can be absorbed, note it in the project team meeting minutes only; there's no need to update the schedule. If this unplanned work is going to be significant or impact the team's ability to continue to execute to the schedule, then it needs to be added to the project schedule. Note that if the work can be absorbed because you've done a great job and added strategic buffers to the schedule, you still need to incorporate this unplanned work into the schedule; it just may not have any impact to the customer commits. To do this, create a separate section in the schedule labeled "Unplanned Work." Under this section, add line items to represent each added task. Be sure to update the schedule logic so that this added work is fully integrated into the workflow. Once this schedule is updated, recommit the final completion date to your stakeholders and save another schedule baseline. This is your new, committed execution timeline. By incorporating this unplanned work into the schedule you have a good way to collect the cumulative effect to the expected release date. Further, you will use this information while reporting out project status during the Execution Phase and in the Closing Phase as you and your team perform a post-release retrospective of the project execution.

Monitoring Metrics

Project execution metrics are perhaps the least understood and most ignored mechanics of the job, so now let's spend some time talking about what you should be tracking and how to use this important data. There are two basic categories of metrics in my mind; Earned Value Management (EVM) metrics and the less sophisticated but no less useful metrics like percentage complete and milestone dates.

If you work in an organization where actual project hours are tracked, then the chances are good that you will be expected to monitor Earned Value (EV) metrics. There are a few formulas that define EVM, so you should take the time to talk to your resident experts and understand exactly how the EVM data is calculated for your organization. These metrics are directly calculated from the data in your project schedule so it's important to keep your schedule current and synch your updates to the publish dates for these metrics. The key to understanding EV metrics is to realize that they are simply ratios of executed work versus planned work. The formulas are fraught with long acronyms for what is essentially a simple formula. Think of EV metrics as the percentage of actual work that was done versus what was planned to be done at a particular point in time. Therefore, an EV metric of less than one means that less work was actually done than you'd planned to be done by that point in time: in other words, you're behind schedule. The flip side is also true; an EV metric of greater than one means that the project is ahead of schedule. Pretty simple, right? EV metrics are calculated on a "per-task" basis, and then the total project EV metrics are weighted averages of all of the individual task EV metrics. The thing that throws many PMs about EV metrics is that they are calculated within the dark depths of your scheduling software, so while your instincts and what your team is telling you indicate that the project is on track, the EV metrics may say that you are behind schedule. This can be frustrating and distracting, especially if your project gets flagged to management as being behind due to "red" EV metrics. As I mentioned, many PMs don't understand the logic behind EVM, so they get stuck when their scheduling software tells them the project is behind schedule yet their gut says that everything is good to go. Having been stuck in this madhouse many times, I can tell you categorically that the scheduling software doesn't lie. So if the EV metrics are less than one, and you think the project is on track, then you need to troubleshoot your schedule logic. To do this, you first verify that all of the work that has been done to date is updated correctly in the schedule. Next, you look for tasks with EV metrics less than one, especially any on the critical path. Are these tasks properly updated? Does the connecting schedule logic look right? What's the task projected finish date and how does it compare to the baseline finish date? Gotcha! If the logic is right, the status is updated, and the projected finish date is beyond the baseline date, then, yes, my friend that task is behind schedule. Sorry . . . I told you that the software doesn't lie. The good news is that if you did a careful job of constructing your schedule as we discussed in Chapter 3, then this troubleshooting is pretty quick and painless. As you can see from walking through the troubleshooting process, EV metrics can be very helpful to the project manager because they give you an overall sense of how closely the work is tracking to the baseline at the project level and they allow you to pinpoint trouble early at the task level. Honestly, the only hard part of EVM is wrapping your brain around the calculations and having a well-constructed project schedule.

Now let's talk about the metrics I monitor for every project, those less sophisticated but still useful ones such as percentage complete and milestone dates. Percentage complete can be a very useful metric despite its limitations which we discussed earlier. Your team and your stakeholders can comprehend exactly what *"60% complete"* means; it's an intuitive and illustrative metric. It's also the easiest metric to get, since its right there in your scheduling software! The other metrics I always monitor are the major milestone dates. If you recall during the schedule development work, we added in milestones to differentiate major work packages. Each of these major milestones can be tracked by comparing the baseline dates with the actual, trending dates. The more these two dates diverge, the further off-track the schedule is. Obviously, if the trend dates are earlier than the baseline dates, that's goodness, whereas trend dates that exceed the baseline dates indicate that a major work package is behind schedule and most likely needs intervention. One of the most useful views in any scheduling software is one which allows the PM to compare these dates in real time, letting you spot troubled tasks before they become major show-stoppers.

Speaking of spotting major show-stoppers early; that's the whole point of collecting this data in the first place! Monitoring these metrics is one of the primary jobs of any PM during the Execution Phase. This work is what PMI refers to as "Monitor and Control." Ironically, I often see junior project managers so distracted by the drama of managing the project that they completely forget about the metrics. That's a mistake because this data is your early warning system. I can tell you the percentage complete and which of the major work packages are trending behind for every project I manage, at any point in time, and you should be able to do that too. Reacting to what the metrics are telling you is a big part of controlling the project, and you can't lead the team to proactively deal with problems if you can't see them coming. This monitoring work is one of the unique values the PM brings to the team. No one else on the project team is looking at performance against the plan and progress toward the customer commit, so it's doubly important that the PM be actively monitoring the project metrics. Monitoring and controlling the project metrics are key factors in leading fire-less, drama-free projects, so if you haven't been paying attention to this data, it really is time to start.

Implementing Risk Reviews

If you will recall, during the Planning Phase you and your team built the project risk register and embedded the risk management plans into your project schedule. For smaller, shorter projects this is sufficient risk management and nothing further needs to be done. However, for larger, longer-duration projects, it's a good practice to review the risk plans and identify any new risks periodically during the Execution Phase of the project work. To do this, you set up a risk review meeting at strategic points in the execution of the project, such as at the completion of major work packages. Consider doing a risk review after the design is completed but before validation starts, for instance.

During these reviews, you want to accomplish two things: review/validate the existing risk management plans and identify any new risks that the team should consider. This can usually be done in an hour but may require more time if the review of the existing risk management plans takes a while. To do this review, as a team step through each of the three to five risks you selected to plan for during Planning. Has a risk been triggered? If the answer is "yes," then assess the adequacy of the risk management plans for that risk. Were they sufficient? Does the team need to do more work? Did new, associated risks pop up as a result of dealing with the original risk? If the risk has not been triggered, are the risk and the plans to deal with it still valid? This review should result in a few action items and possibly some new tasks to add into the schedule. These tasks should be tracked under the "Unplanned Work" section of your schedule.

Next, as a team, review the risks you originally identified but chose to accept rather than plan for. Are there any risks that the team needs to take seriously now? Brainstorm as a team to come up with new risks that you didn't originally consider. Rate and rank these new risks just like you did during the Planning Phase. As a team, decide whether or not you need to address more risks, always keeping in mind the available bandwidth of the team. Remember, the keys to realistic risk management are to limit the additional work your teammates need to do by limiting the number of risks they address and by embedding the tasks into the project schedule. Do not inadvertently overload your teammates by committing to more risk management activities than the team can reasonably do. At the end of the risk review, update your risk register and update the project schedule by placing any new tasks under the "Unplanned Work" section. Repeat this review process as many times as seems reasonable for the duration of the project. Yes, I realize that "as seems reasonable" is rather fuzzy, but there really are no hard-and-fast rules here. You have to use your judgment and consider when the team has time to do this work. Consider these reviews as preventative maintenance for the project work and fit them in on a regular cadence.

Generate Project Status Report-Outs

Reporting out the status of your project is one of the expected project management tasks, and while there's a certain amount of "art" to the work, there are some basic mechanics you should understand. In my first book, *Managing Projects in the Real World* (Apress, 2013), I spent an entire chapter on this artistry, but here we will focus on the basics, the mechanics of building a status report. One purpose of these report-outs is to communicate the project status to a larger audience, but an even more important and primary purpose is to manage your stakeholders' expectations. Therefore, the content should provide the consumer of this information with a clear picture of the project work at that point in time. It should answer these key questions: is the work on track, are there any changes to the Plan of Record (POR), and is there any help needed. Because this information is consumed by a broad audience, many of whom are key stakeholders, it's important that it be accurate and properly curated.

The first question that comes to mind is what information needs to be included. The status report must include those execution metrics you are monitoring which we discussed above. Simply state *"The project is 78% complete."* You should also include EVM metrics if those are well understood by your status report consumers. It should be noted that while the project management community within your organization may deeply understand these metrics, the rank and file may not. The report-out must also contain the trend dates for the major milestones and customer commits. It is a best practice to include the baseline/commit dates plus the trending dates for only the specific milestones your status consumers care about, which will be a subset of the major milestones you track within your schedule. These dates plus the execution metrics are the quantitative data of your status report. Quantitative data points are great for representing project status because they lend credibility to your overall update and demonstrate that you are actively monitoring and controlling the project execution. Other quantitative date to consider including in your report are things like defect statistics, conversion rates, user acceptance metrics, budget data, buffer consumption, etc. Beyond the quantitative data, the status report must include a brief summary of any highlights, lowlights, potential risks to the project, key decisions, help needed, and next steps. This information should be timely and succinct; representing the work that has been done since the last report-out. In addition to these elements, I typically include a stoplight graphic (green, yellow, red) to represent my subjective assessment of the state of the project taking into account all of the forces in play. This provides the status consumers with a quick assessment of whether the project is on track (green), in jeopardy (yellow), or missing commit (red). This is a lot of information to convey, and the key to successfully communicating your project status lies in keeping the update succinct and at an appropriate level of detail for the audience.

Once you understand what information you need to communicate with your status report, it's time to think about what format would be most appropriate. When deciding what format to use, you need to take into account any organizational requirements, how your stakeholders prefer to communicate, and how this information will be utilized. In organizations with mature project management practices it's likely that you will be required to provide your status data via a specific tool. In more informal organizations a brief e-mail is often sufficient. Some organizations prefer to make use of online collaboration tools, so you may find yourself posting your status to an online forum or blog. If your status report consumers will be embedding your update into broader presentations, then it might make sense to construct your update in a PowerPoint format. The thing to remember here is that the format doesn't matter; what matters is that the information be accurate, clear, and succinct. I should also point out that it may be necessary to develop your project status in more than one format, depending on the needs of your key stakeholders. (Figure 4-1)

Project Management Basics
Summary: Project is 43% complete; continuing to make progress as planned; no issues.

Key Milestones				Highlights:
Milestone	Plan	Trend	Actual	• Submitted first draft of Ch 3
Project Start	12/20	-	12/20	• First draft of Ch 4 50%
1st Draft Comp	7/16	6/1	-	
Editing Comp	8/15	8/15	-	
Final Proof	10/1	10/1	-	
Book Published	10/15	10/15	-	

Remaining Schedule Buffer: 3 weeks

Lowlights:
Missed a drawing for Ch 3; plan to complete this next week

Plans for next week:
- Submit first draft of Ch4
- Complete 50% of Ch5 first draft

Risks:
- Weeklong buisness trip at the end of the month; limited ablity to work on this project while traveling

Key Decisions:
Complete first draft manuscript before summer vacation (6/1)

Figure 4-1. Project status report example

Stage Escalations

New project managers often shy away from deliberately escalating issues due to a desire to stay "under the radar," when in fact it's their job to resolve any roadblocks impending the project execution. I would go so far as to say that this is one of their most important jobs as project team leaders, and failing to escalate is failing the team. So how do you escalate an issue to remove a roadblock anyway? Oh, and it would be nice to be able to do this without bringing down a world of hurt on your head, right?

There are a few tricks to effectively escalating issues. First, it's all about the data. If you've had trouble escalating issues in the past, take a look at the supporting data you provided. Is it quantitative, accurate, and clear? If not, well, there's your trouble. To be effective at escalating issues, you need to provide supporting data that is conclusive and quantitative, so go off and find that as a first step. The second trick to effective escalation is this: escalate the effect not the cause (i.e., address the impact of the crappy deliverable versus the slacker providing that deliverable). Here you want to go with something like *"Unfortunately, we've found ten more defects with the CAD files, which has delayed the board availability 2 full weeks"* instead of *"Melanie is doing such a sloppy job on the layout that we have to go back and rework everything she delivers."* The first statement is quantitative and addresses the real problem for the project team, whereas the second is unsubstantiated and sounds like whining. It's always more effective to position the issue around the consequences of someone's actions than it is to directly criticize that person. The third "trick" to effective escalation is to have a recommendation in your back pocket. It's naïve to go to the decision-makers and say *"Hey, you know we are behind schedule, so we need more heads to be able to deliver to our original customer commit"* and expect any help. Instead, you need to provide the data to the decision-makers; that is, you need to tell them how to solve the problem. Don't expect them to divine the best course of action on the fly, during a confrontational meeting. At a minimum, you need to articulate a couple of options for solving the problem so that those decision-makers can make a call; after all, you and your team are the subject matter experts here, right? Finally, the last trick, and honestly it's the most important, is to remain professional. Getting angry or frustrated doesn't help and in fact can serve to inflame the discussion further. Present your issue, the supporting data, and the team's recommendations in a calm manner and stay above the hissing and spitting your less-evolved colleagues indulge in. If you do these things, then your chances of positively resolving the roadblock go up dramatically. The hard part of escalating issues is the soft skills challenges; laying the groundwork by collecting the data and developing alternatives is the easy part. Here's another case where the mechanics of the job are easy, so master them to give yourself more time and mental bandwidth to deal with the soft skills challenges.

Checklist #3—The Execution Phase

The Execution Phase of the project is where all of that planning you did in Chapter 3 gets applied. In this phase, project managers create artifacts in the service of performing the project work; these artifacts include change requests, meeting minutes, and project status updates. Here you also maintain the schedule and risk register by regularly updating them as the work evolves. Checklist 3 is a bit different from the previous two you've used because these items are recurring, meaning that you will do these tasks multiple times throughout this phase. The important thing to keep in mind is that you should be doing all of these tasks; they represent the minimum tasks you need to perform during Execution.

Checklist #3—The Execution Phase

☐ Standing team meetings are effective and held regularly with a stated agenda

☐ Changes to the POR are managed effectively through the project and program-level CCBs

☐ The project schedule is updated regularly, incorporating unplanned work as needed

☐ Project execution metrics have been established, are monitored regularly, and drive corrective actions as needed

☐ Project risks are reviewed regularly with new risks identified and action plans updated as needed

☐ Project status updates are provided to key stakeholders at a regular cadence

☐ Problems impeding the team's ability to execute the project plan are efficiently escalated

The Execution Phase is the longest phase of the project lifecycle, and you will find yourself regularly performing the tasks we've discussed and updating the artifacts you originally created during planning all throughout this phase. Typically, this phase represents 60–70% of the total project duration, so you'll be hanging out here a while. It's a good idea to drop a couple of placeholders onto your work calendar to remind yourself to go do some of these tasks such as the risk reviews so that they don't drop through the cracks. For other tasks, such as producing the project status updates, you will find yourself falling into a regular cadence naturally. Next we will move into releasing your project deliverables and closing out the project.

Releasing Your First Project

If you will recall, in Chapter 4 I mentioned that the Execution Phase of any project is the longest. In fact you should think of the Execution Phase as having two parts; one part of the work is the execution of the project work and the other is the actual release of the project deliverables. Traditional project management training materials gloss over, or completely ignore, the second part because it's such a small part of the overall execution of the project work. Here's the thing: the release work is the home stretch, the last mile, the final shot, the last piece of chicken, etc., and if your team chokes on the release it's entirely possible to turn what was a successful project into a hot mess with a bad reputation. So as a project manager, how do you avoid that career-deadening move? You carefully plan for, and execute, the release of the deliverables, and I'm going to show you just how to do that here.

© Melanie McBride 2016

M. McBride, *Project Management Basics*, DOI 10.1007/978-1-4842-2086-3_5

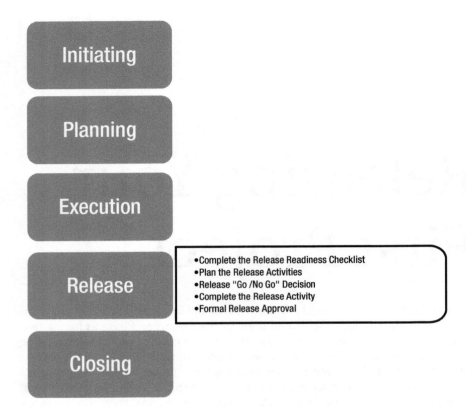

Initiating

Planning

Execution

Release
- Complete the Release Readiness Checklist
- Plan the Release Activities
- Release "Go /No Go" Decision
- Complete the Release Activity
- Formal Release Approval

Closing

To avoid becoming the poster child for "Help Needed," you need to leverage the work you and your team did in the Planning Phase and those relationships with your key stakeholders that you've nurtured all through the Execution Phase. Here I'll walk you through how to use that Release Readiness Checklist you built in Planning, we'll refine the release approval decision criteria, I'll walk you through what you need to do to get that approval, and we'll talk a bit about how to plan that execution. You see, a well-planned, carefully executed release plan is a critical component of any successful project.

DIALING DOWN THE DRAMA

Apart from a major risk being triggered, there's no other situation in the project lifecycle more stressful and drama-inducing than the release activities. This is the point in time where the project team's work has to stand alone: it's their professional reputation on the line and no one wants to hear that their baby is ugly. Further, your major stakeholders have a vested interest in a successful release, so they are going to be all up in your business if you're not careful. Mix a bunch of people with their professional reputations at stake with a tight timeline and you're bound to get some major drama that will negatively impact both your team's ability to execute and your reputation as a leader.

So, how do you avoid a Wild West show of a release and instead turn it into something as sedate and controlled as doing your laundry? First, you start with your demeanor and project calm confidence. The team will follow your lead here, so if you run around like your hair is on fire because someone forgot to post the Marketing collateral, then chances are your team will behave similarly. Second, you work with your team to develop a solid release plan, carefully laying out who needs to do what and when it must get done. Often, these release plans are more detailed than the project schedule, but that's okay, because in this instance, the team needs to understand exactly what work will be done, possibly down to the hour or minute. Third, you must control the messaging so that what your stakeholders hear is what you want them to know, namely, that the release work is progressing and it's on track to an actual plan. By this point in the project, since you've been following, and refining, that communication plan you built during Planning, you have a good handle on what your key stakeholders care about. Don't leave this to chance and don't let someone else co-opt the reputation of your project team at this point in the game.

Do these three things and even if your release activities encounter major problems, your team will be able to focus on solving the problems instead of riding an emotional roller coaster that's about to jump the tracks. The goal here is to orchestrate a release event so smooth and controlled that it's almost boring in its execution. Let me give you a real-world example of what I'm talking about. Take your average high school graduation ceremony. Here's a case where the participants are wildly excited and barely paying attention to what's going on. The high school staff executing the event, on the other hand, know exactly what to do and when it needs to happen. They are calm and in control of the event. What could have been utter madness is instead mind-numbingly boring, except for that brief moment when "your" student walks across the stage. That's what you're aiming for, a release event so smoothly executed it's almost boring, and the only way to get there is to actively dial down the drama.

Assessing the Release Readiness

Now it's time to get into the nuts and bolts of that "carefully executed" release plan, and we start with an old friend, the Release Readiness Checklist. If you will recall, you developed this checklist during the Planning Phase, back in Chapter 3. This checklist consists of those items deemed to be absolutely required. It represents the due diligence your team has done to ensure that the deliverable is safe, legal, and compliant. Basically what you will do now is go through the checklist and ensure that each item has been completed, but there are a few nuances with respect to how you actually do this, so that's what we'll talk about next.

You want to review your Release Readiness Checklist early enough to have time to go back and complete anything that has slipped through the cracks but late enough in the Execution Phase that the majority of the work is completed. Exactly when this should be done is a bit tricky, and you will get a better feel for it as you gain experience. For now, since you baked each of these items into your project schedule, aim to do a first-pass review of the checklist 3 to 4 weeks prior to the release activity. One week before you plan to do the review, send the Release Readiness Checklist out to your team and assign them the task to complete their sections prior to the team meeting in the following week. Sure, not everyone will actually do this task, but it's a good policy to give them the opportunity to excel. Use that block of time in your weekly team meeting agenda reserved for special topics to review the Release Readiness Checklist and tick off any items that have been completed. Specifically note when any open items will be closed and who owns that work in the checklist. It's common for there to be a few open items when you do this first review, so don't worry, just continue to review this checklist in your standing team meetings until all items are closed. Note that any item that cannot be completed should be considered a "show-stopper" and its resolution should be your top priority at this point in the project. Explicit stakeholder approval that the release can go forward without all items on the checklist completed is needed before the actual release activity kicks off. If you can't get this approval, then it's your responsibility as the project manager to postpone the release until this matter can be resolved. Since these items are considered to be the bare minimum due diligence requirements, it's a matter of professional integrity that you not allow the release to go forward until each item is completed or appropriate waivers have been obtained.

Plan the Release

Now that you have the Release Readiness Checklist in hand, it's time to turn your attention to developing a plan for the release activities. Teams do this in a variety of ways, so there are no hard and fast rules here. The basic idea is to figure out all of the release tasks and when they need to be done. You and your team can do this with a simple spreadsheet, a complicated schedule, or something in the middle. Often, the project collateral dictates the release process, or your organization may have specific requirements that outline the steps the release activity has to take. If you're not sure where to start, consider developing a WBS and a Network Diagram just like you did when you built your project schedule. To do this, get your team together and first identify all of the release tasks, then lay them out in an efficient flow. It's important to get your team's buy-in to the workflow so that everyone is on the same page about what needs to be done. Now that you've got the release workflow identified, consider whether or not you need to coordinate with other teams. It's not uncommon to need an upstream or downstream team to provide inputs or validate outputs of your project deliverables.

After you've figured out the work of the release and how long it should take, it's time to schedule these activities. As you calendar the release activities, consider who the required personnel are, and who only needs to be aware of the work going on. You may need to send out two separate notices: a calendar item for the folks actually doing the work and a "for your information" e-mail to let interested stakeholders know when the release work will be done. As you go about setting these events up, pay careful attention to who must participate and be sure to confirm that these critical people are going to be available. The last thing you want to happen is a delay in the release work because a critical participant has to leave early to pick up their child from soccer practice. It's a good practice to verify one last time, the day before, that each of the critical players is planning to attend. Remember, you want your release activities to be so well coordinated that the actual execution seems boring.

Finally, be sure to arrange any logistics needed for the release. Do you need to reserve lab space or a large conference room? If the team will be working through lunch or long into the night, do you need to arrange for food to be brought in? Establish a communication plan for the release itself, making sure that those critical stakeholders know when and how they will get updates on the release work. Create an update communication template so that in the fury of the release activity, all you have to do is pull up that template and start typing. Draft up a couple of announcements that you can send out if the release goes well and if it tanks. Having these drafts in your back pocket makes it much easier to quickly craft concise, well-written updates even if the release activities are grueling.

Confirming Your Go/No Go Criteria

Okay, now we're going to backtrack a little and make sure that all of the key stakeholders are in agreement about what constitutes a successful release. In a perfect world, the project success criteria are requirements that explicitly spell out quantifiable metrics that, if achieved, warrant a "Go" decision on the release of the project deliverables. Stop rolling your eyes! I get it! You don't work in that "perfect" world; you work in the real world where requirements are squishy and the ecosystem can change dramatically over the course of the project, which is why you need to do a little backtracking here. This is the time to meet with each of your major stakeholders and confirm that your understanding of the release approval criteria matches theirs and that each stakeholder is aligned with their fellow stakeholders.

Now there's an efficient way to do this and then there's the effective way to go about it. It can seem more efficient to handle this task with an e-mail or a meeting. In my experience, the e-mail just doesn't work, since you will either get no thoughtful responses or instigate a dialog that meanders around and doesn't conclusively confirm the understanding of the "Go" criteria. Holding a meeting is a crapshoot; it can be extremely effective if all of the major stake-holders attend and engage in the discussion. Unfortunately, this kind of meet-ing can be challenging to organize logistically and has the potential to turn into a venue for interoffice politics that have little to do with your project. It's far more effective to have informal conversations with each of your major stakeholders. You should already be meeting with these people on a regular basis, so sometime before the release, as part of your regular update to these stakeholders, verify that criteria for a "Go" decision.

To be honest, if you've been actively managing your stakeholders' expectations and impressions of the project work, then there's very little to do here. It's a good idea to do this sort of backchannel confirmation prior to the actual release approval so that there are no surprises at the last minute. Remember, your goal is to have a boring, completely predictable release, so don't leave this understanding of what will get your team that "Go" decision to chance.

Executing the Release

By this point in time, all of the Release Readiness Checklist items are com-pleted, the team has a plan to execute the release, and all of your decision-makers are aligned on what constitutes success for the release. It's time to rock and roll! If you and your team have developed a solid plan for the release activities, then chances are there's very little for you, as the project manager, to do. Your job now is to enable the team to execute the release. This is an important point, so let's elaborate on it a bit. Your job now is to make sure the work happens by removing roadblocks, ensuring that the team has the resources they need to do the work, and, frankly, keeping management off their backs by providing regular updates. *Your job is not to do the actual work of releasing the deliverable,* that is, it's not to troubleshoot that installer bug or hang out at the back of the lab offering "helpful" suggestions on what to do next. You are the conductor of your motley crew, not that overly enthusiastic tuba player, so stay out of their way and let them do what they do best.

The trick then is to remain available to your team, quietly smoothing the way behind the scenes. One of the best ways to do this is to actively manage the team morale. Kick off the release activities with your team by giving them a little pep talk. Remind them of all of the work they've done, express your confidence that they are up to any challenge that comes their way during the release, and let them know that you will be there to remove any roadblocks. This is an excellent time to dial down the drama and infuse the team with a sense of purpose, so don't miss this opportunity because you're uncomfort-able doing these kinds of morale builders. It may feel hokey to you, and it may seem hokey to some of your teammates, but trust me, doing this definitely impacts how the release activities will proceed.

To actively manage your team's morale, pay attention to how things are going and how the team interacts. If things start slipping and the tension is ratcheting up, then perhaps it's time to break for lunch. It's a good idea to introduce some small break every couple of hours so that your team has the chance to mentally recover, especially if the work is particularly intense. Obviously, you don't want to distract them, but you can often lighten the mood and provide that mental break simply by checking in to see how things are going. Finally, if the work is going badly, the team is frustrated, and team members are starting to turn on each other, then it's time to step in and actively dial down the drama. Refocus the team on a plan of action with specific tasks so that they can start making progress on solving whatever problems are blocking the execution of the release plan. This is when you need to manage the stakeholders and the messaging so that the team can focus on their work instead of that screaming director who wants someone's head on a pike. All of these behind-the-scenes actions matter; they are what make that boring, well-executed release possible.

Gaining Release Approval

Final approval for your project release can come at several different points in the project lifecycle, and when it happens is dependent on your particular organization. Some organizations have a formal approval process that happens before the team can start the release activities, some hold the approval to the end of the release, while others require approval at both points in time. No matter when it happens, there are a few things you need to do. You will be expected to present evidence that due diligence was done and that the requirements of the project are fulfilled by the deliverables and associated release process. This is the easy part and typically consists of getting on the agenda of the approval board, submitting a change request, and completing some checklist or form; it may also require you to pull together a presentation. Remember, you incorporated these approval criteria in your project plan during Planning, so all that's really left is to share the evidence that this work was done. That's the formal part of the work, and if your organization is very mature with respect to project management, then this process is well documented. I'll specifically address what to do if no such approval process exists later in Chapter 7.

That's the formal process for gaining release approval; now let's talk about the *informal* but no less important process. Similar to what you did earlier to confirm the "Go for release" criteria, you want to sit down with each of the release approval decision-makers to review the project work and the deliverables. The goal is to make sure that each person is comfortable approving the release ahead of the actual release decision. If any of the stakeholders have concerns about the release, now's the time to go address them. Since these are the people you've spent the life of the project building relationships with, these should be easy and comfortable discussions. Infrequently, a few stakeholders will have issues with the release whose resolutions are mutually exclusive. Here's where you need to take action. To end run this potential gate to the release approval, set up a separate meeting with the stakeholders who are not aligned. Open the meeting by asking for their help to resolve the issue, stressing the fact that their misalignment is gating factor for successfully completing the project. It's important for the project manager to remain neutral here and provide the facts for these decision-makers. If asked for a recommendation, state your position and back it up with quantifiable data. The objective here is to get these stakeholders to resolve their differences without impacting the project team. If you take care of these disconnects and preload approvals with your stakeholders, then the release approval becomes nothing more than a rubber stamp, which is exactly what you're aiming for, isn't it?

Holding the Go/No Go Meeting

There are some subtle differences between the formal release approval and a "Go/No Go" decision, so let me break them down for you now. The formal release approval is just that: formal. It's also the point in time where you prove that your team has done due diligence and that the deliverables meet the expected outcomes. This approval frequently comes before the actual release activity. There are documented processes and approval boards you must satisfy to release your project deliverables. "Go/No Go" decisions are used a bit differently.

There are two scenarios where you find this type of decision. In the first, there's less organizational structure around release approvals, so you would use a "Go/No Go" decision point to put some formality into the approval to release. I'll talk more about this particular use in Chapter 7. The second scenario where you find "Go/No Go" decision-making is within the project team. Here each team member provides their recommendations to a decision-maker who then makes a decision on whether or not they are ready to proceed with the release activities. As you can imagine, these types of decisions are fairly easy to facilitate but you should keep in mind that these are important project decisions, so there's bound to be a lot of emotional investment in the outcome.

When facilitating a "Go/No Go" meeting, it's best to follow a strict process to help dial down the drama and keep the discussion focused on the main topic of the meeting, whether or not the release is approved. Follow the decision-making methodology the team agreed to during the Initiating Phase. For consultative decision-making, it looks like this. Start the meeting by having the most senior team member who was involved in the release work summarize the release activities. Next, go "around the table" and collect recommendations from each team member. Each recommender is to provide their "Go/No Go" recommendation, and if the recommendation is "No Go," then they must provide their primary concern. Actively facilitate the discussion to limit the discussion to the recommendation and primary concerns; do not allow it to drift into problem-solving or finger-pointing. If necessary, reiterate the purpose of the meeting, which is to reach a release decision, and let the team know that anything else will be addressed in a separate meeting. The project manager should provide their recommendation to the decision-maker last, and then ask for any questions. After any questions have been answered to the decision-maker's satisfaction, they should make the "Go/No Go" decision.

Communicating the Release Status

During the release activity, you need to keep your key stakeholders informed of the work and how it's progressing. It's a rookie mistake to "go dark" during the release because the rumor mill will be working overtime and you need to be in front of any negative impressions that will affect your team's ability to problem-solve and complete the work. While planning for the release, you figured out how often, and in what format, you would provide regular updates, so all you really need to do is execute that communication plan.

While writing up the status report, take care to manage the information you provide; it should be at the appropriate level of detail for your key stakeholders and it should be actionable by them. Spare these senior leaders the gory details of the hoops the team had to jump through to install the application because the documentation was crap; instead, simply mention that "the application was successfully installed and some documentation updates were identified." By providing regular updates, you are doing two key things: first, you are establishing that your team has a plan and that they know what they are doing, and second, by communicating openly and regularly you are building trust with these stakeholders. Nothing escalates an already floundering release like the impression that the team has no clue how to solve an unexpected show-stopper defect or that it is actively hiding information. Remember, your goal is a boring, predictable release, so just do yourself and the team a favor and send out regular updates.

Once the "Go/No Go" decision is made, then you need to let everyone affected know. Here you only need to pull up that pre-written announcement you created while planning the release, tweak the wording a bit, and hit "send." If the release went badly and the decision was "No Go," then summarize what was accomplished, succinctly describe the show-stopper issue, and clearly articulate the next steps the team will take. Finally, be sure to both thank those who have assisted the team so far and specifically ask for any help needed to execute those next steps. If the release was successfully boring, then summarize what was accomplished, reiterate the business impact or value this project enables, and be sure to thank the team and your stakeholders for a successful release.

Okay, right now you're probably thinking something like *"Gee that sure is a lot of hand-holding. I don't see why I have to pander to my stakeholders that much and of course I'm going to be in the middle of troubleshooting any bugs during the release.*" Here's the thing: if you really want to execute that predictably boring release, then yes, you really do need to do all of that work. These backchannel conversations that preload the release approval and that ability to enable your team without having to be the one to identify the root cause of that monster bug are what separates the often-successful project managers from the rock stars. It's a matter of initiative and effort. Remember, your job as the project manager is to enable the team to execute, which means that you need to make sure that they have the space, both physical and mental, to do their best work. By laying the groundwork for that predictable, boring release, you are actually helping your team go faster. Trust them to handle the troubleshooting while you handle management. This is one of the easiest ways to improve your project management effectiveness, so if you've struggled to get through project releases in the past, next time create an actual release plan and focus on stakeholder management while your team takes care of the actual release activities. I think you'll be pleasantly surprised with the results.

Checklist #4—Releasing the Project Deliverables

The release work in the Execution Phase is a special subset of the work you do to execute the project. Here you leveraged the work done in the Planning Phase to evaluate whether or not the team is ready to release the project deliverable. You pave the way with your major stakeholders to ensure that the release approval is "in the bag" as long as the release activities go well. You enable your team to complete the release activities by establishing and maintaining a low-drama environment. Finally, you successfully navigate the release approval process. The following checklist identifies the major tasks you need to complete as you lead your team to release the project deliverables. The important thing to keep in mind is that you should be doing all of these tasks; they represent the minimum tasks you need to perform during the release process.

Checklist #4—Releasing the Project Deliverables

☐ Ensure all items on the Release Readiness Checklist have been completed

☐ For Release Readiness Checklist items that cannot be completed prior to the release, obtain the necessary waivers and stakeholder approval prior to the release

☐ Complete the release plan (all work identified and organized into a logical flow, event scheduled, communication plan ready)

☐ Confirm release approval/"Go/No Go" decision criteria with key stakeholders

☐ Complete release activity

☐ Obtain formal release approval

☐ Provide formal notification of release status to key stakeholders

---

Congratulations! You've just completed the execution of your project and wrapped up the bulk of the project work! It's all over but the cryin' now. You and your team have developed and executed a plan to release the project deliverables. Because you worked diligently to leverage those stakeholder relationships you've been building, the release approval was smooth and anticlimactic. Good job! You have one last bit of work to complete, and that's officially closing out the project, which we'll address next, in Chapter 6.

Closing Your First Project

By now you should be feeling pretty good; you and your team have success-fully released the project deliverables and the project is practically over. All that remains to do is the closure activities, so hang on for a few more check-list items, which once completed, will allow you to pull an Elvis . . . and leave the building! There's actually not much work to be done during Closing, but the work there is needs to be done in a timely manner. To properly close the project, you and your team need to review the team's performance and iden-tify areas of improvement for future projects. You will do that by facilitating a project retrospective. You also need to ensure that your team cleans house by disposing of leftover material, publishing any collateral that may still be out-standing, and making sure that all of the project work is appropriately archived. As part of closing down the project, you will also need to create a project summary and review it with your key stakeholders to ensure that each one agrees that all of the committed project work is complete. Finally, you need to take care of your team by formally recognizing their accomplishments and celebrating the successful release. Note that unlike the other project lifecycle phases, much of the closing work is done simultaneously and is quick to com-plete. Depending on how complicated your project is, you should expect to spend 1 to 2 weeks closing out the project. Getting this work done before the team is fully involved in another project is the hardest challenge for this phase of the project, so you will need to execute the Closing work as quickly as possible. Let's break down what you need to do.

© Melanie McBride 2016

M. McBride, *Project Management Basics*, DOI 10.1007/978-1-4842-2086-3_6

Initiating

Planning

Execution

Release

Closing

- •Conduct a Project Retrospective
- •Disposition Leftover HW
- •Archive SW and Documentation
- •Publish Project Summary
- •Obtain agreement that the project work is complete
- •Celebrate the project completion
- •Recognize the team
- •Release resources from the project

Facilitate a Project Retrospective

Any organization that has some project management infrastructure in place will expect you to do a proper project retrospective at the end of the project. Some organizations even require this at each phase gate. Further, it really is a best practice for the team to step back and dispassionately review their work to identify areas of improvement to carry forward to future projects. This process goes by many names ("Lessons Learned," "Retrospective," "Post Mortem," etc.), but these all describe essentially the same beast, and it's likely that you are already familiar with them. Essentially, the objective here is for the team to review their performance relative to their plan to identify what worked well, what needs improvement, and any key learnings they need to pass along to other teams doing similar work. This is actually a pretty straightforward activity, but it does require some preparation by the project manager, so let's talk about that next.

To run a productive retrospective, you need to do some upfront work. First, pull together the project metrics to provide some insight into how thorough the planning work was. Create a table of the major milestones with their planned completion dates, their actual completion dates, and any relevant notes. Note that you want to compare your original plan with your actual outcome. Now go dig around in your schedule notes and meeting minutes to understand any differences between these two dates. It's not uncommon to replan or adjust the commitments for these dates as the project progresses, so it's okay for there to be some variation in these milestone dates. What you're really looking for here is why those dates vary. This will tell you and your team a lot about how good your plan really was. For example, did you miss the "Design Complete" milestone by 3 weeks? Could that be due to the fact that you had a large number of change requests from the program? If so, then that's actually useful information for planning the next project that supports the same program. Next time, you'll add some buffer for change requests initiated at the program level. It's also useful feedback for the program team, allowing them to comprehend the impact of their CCB decisions. Next, pull in any other project metrics you've been tracking and do a similar analysis. To understand how much the scope of work changed, review your change log and see if there are some major changes or trends that help explain any differences between the planned scope of work and what was actually delivered. To evaluate the effectiveness of your risk management planning, review the risk register generated in the Planning Phase and consider how well the risk management plans worked. Other good metrics to look into are effort, a.k.a. "hours," and any validation metrics you tracked as part of controlling the project execution. As you can see, there's quite a bit of data out there to pull from, so this is mostly an exercise in data mining. The important thing to keep in mind here is that you should let the data speak for itself. Be objective when collecting this information and be open to whatever it's telling you. For instance, it's entirely possible to deliver something your customer absolutely loves but whose execution was extremely messy and took significantly longer than expected. Is that project a success? I don't know, but it's definitely something the team should dissect during the retrospective.

The actual retrospective meeting can be done in the same timeslot as your standing team update meetings; just devote the entire meeting to this topic. As you schedule the retrospective, pay attention to who accepts the meeting invite. It's very important to the overall quality of the output that each functional area be represented and that your core team contributes to the discussion. If key players can't attend the meeting, then reschedule it to a better time. The most important thing here is that you hold this meeting as soon after the release as possible; shoot for 1 to 2 weeks out from the release activity. To conduct the retrospective, start by walking through the metrics and data you collected up front. Keep this part of the discussion objective and let the data speak for itself. This does two important things. First, it level-sets the team on the scope of the discussion. This is important because your team is probably still ruminating over the release activity, and as we know that's only a small part of the project work. Reviewing the metrics helps reset everyone to consider the execution of the entire project. The second thing reviewing the data up front often does is to uncover trends that the team missed in the fog of war. For instance, it's common for the team to simply not see the amount of unplanned work they've knocked out or understand how long the project spent in a "red" state. Reviewing this data helps the entire team appreciate the work that was done and the obstacles that were overcome. Now comes the brainstorming portion of the program. Walk your team through brainstorming what went particularly well for this project, then segue into what did not go well. Care should be taken to actively facilitate this discussion, as you will find that your team is quite passionate about these items. You need to ensure that everyone gets the chance to contribute while maintaining a collaborative team dynamic. Next, discuss the key learnings: those things that need to be passed along to other teams or incorporated into established processes to improve future performance. You will publish those key learnings as part of the final project summary, which we will cover later in this chapter. Finally, end the discussion on a high note by congratulating the team on everything they achieved. This is doubly important if the release was difficult, and really, isn't that how you'd like to be treated as well? The goal here is to leave this team feeling like winners. A big part of project leadership is the ability to motivate and influence your teammates, so don't let them walk away from this project with negative associations about the project or your leadership abilities. You will likely work with these people again, and ending this project on a high note will go a long way to enhancing your ability to motivate and influence them in the future. Ideally, you want them to be excited about the next project because you are leading it.

Clean House

A big part of the closing activities revolves around cleaning house, and by that I mean putting things back where they belong. There's likely to be leftover hardware, discs full of code, collateral that needs to be published to its final resting place, architecture and assorted design documentation that all needs to be dealt with, etc. Fail to put this stuff up and you'll create problems down the road for other teams. I'd bet my lunch money that you've had the experience of working on a new project where some piece of documentation about the product is out of date or just flat-out missing. Kinda frustrating, isn't it? Luckily, this is a quick and easy thing to take care of while you and your team are closing out the project.

One lesson I learned early in my career is that hardware leftover from a project acts like *Star Trek* Tribbles; it multiplies like rabbits when you're not looking and soon you're getting nasty notes exhorting you to get those boxes out of your cube because they've now become a fire hazard. Have your team do a clean-up of their office and lab spaces, appropriately dispositioning this material so that it doesn't have a chance to breed. If the project involves a lot of leftover hardware, assign someone to collect the leftover material and process it for scrap, reintroduce it into inventory, or find some other home for it. Software projects tend to generate a lot of CDs, USB drives, and files on servers that are no longer needed. Have your team members do a scrub of this data and clean this up as well. Send a note to your team asking that each person archive any important project data. Have someone double-check that all of the project collateral has been moved to its permanent home. In short, set the expectation with your team that everyone cleans up after themselves. These will be the last of the project tasks they have to complete.

Publish a Project Summary

It's now time to summarize the entire project, and that can be a daunting task. The goal of the project summary is to provide a "soundbite"-worthy story that describes what your project team accomplished. You will use this summary to ensure that your key stakeholders agree that all of the project work is done, you and your teammates will incorporate pieces of the summary into your annual performance reviews, and perhaps most importantly, it's your final bit of project PR, so it's important to take the time to craft a well-written message.

Start with a brief explanation of what the team achieved, and remember to keep this focused on the business objectives that were met by the project deliverables. Next, summarize the data you pulled together for the retrospective. This data should adequately explain the scope of work and the cost to execute it (hours, budget, etc.). Keep this part of the summary data-based and objective. Finally, wrap up the summary with another brief explanation; this time, cover what the successful completion of this project enables and why it matters to the organization, the company, and its customers. Remember, this should be a "soundbite," not *Beowulf*, so keep it short, sweet, and data driven.

Close Out with Your Key Stakeholders

Once you have a well-crafted summary, you need to review it with the key stakeholders and gain their agreement that the work is complete. This is actually a very important step that's easy to forget or blow off. Unfortunately, if you don't confirm that each of the key stakeholders agrees that the work is complete, you run the risk of owning a project that just won't die. Here's what happens. Two months later you get a call from one of those stakeholders asking you to have the project team tweak a deliverable or do some further work. Unfortunately, by this time, all of your team members have been reassigned to other work and are no longer available. You're going to have to tell this stakeholder "no," and that's going to create problems with no easy solution for you. Do yourself and your teammates a favor by meeting with each stakeholder one last time to confirm that they agree the project is completed and that any further work would need to be requested and funded separately. Since you've spent the entire project meeting regularly with these folks, this is another easy discussion to have, and it serves as a nice excuse for one last check-in with these stakeholders to ensure that they have a positive impression of you, your team, and the work you've done.

One thing to keep in mind as you are closing out the project with your key stakeholders is that you want to continue these professional relationships long after this project is put to bed. These people are now part of your professional network, and you can tap them for advice, resources, or opportunities as long as you take the time to maintain the connection. It's always a good idea to let these people know that you enjoyed working with them and that you're receptive to helping them out in the future. In some cases, you may want to set up a more formal mentorship or even just a standing lunch date once a month to keep the connection going. You've spent the entire project nurturing these relationships, so don't let them go once the project is over. In our highly matrixed world, having a robust and diverse network is a key success factor for anyone but especially for project managers, who are constantly looking for ways to enable their teams.

Take Care of Your Team

There's one more area you need to concern yourself with as you wrap up your project, and that's taking care of your team. These people have followed where you led, done tremendous work, and expect you to acknowledge it. How you recognize your team at this point in the project goes a long way to enhancing your ability to motivate and lead these same people on future projects, so make sure that you are taking care of your team during the Closing Phase.

It's important to celebrate the completion of the project with your team. This does two important things; first, it provides a visible and tangible recognition of the work the team has done, and second, it provides a sense of closure, which is particularly important for long projects. Celebrations can be tricky to execute in part due to organizational culture and budget limitations. It's important to note that these celebrations don't have to be elaborate or expensive. I've held project celebrations with nothing more than some cheap takeout pizza and a few words from key stakeholders in a conference room over lunch. If the organization isn't willing to pay for it, I'll dip into my own pocket to pay for those pizzas. This is not about getting free lunch out of my boss; it's about recognizing the hard work the team has done and laying the groundwork for more and better collaboration with these people in the future. Sure, it may require a little more creativity on your part if your team is virtual, but even then is likely that you already know another colleague who can help you out here. I partner with a fellow PM colleague located at another site who is willing to bring in treats for my team members there, and I do the same for his team members located at my site. If you've got access to a more generous budget, then go for it. The important thing here is to take the time to celebrate the team's work. Trust me, your team will appreciate any gesture and they will definitely notice if their work seems to be taken for granted. Don't forget the value in having those key stakeholders come meet the team and express their congratulations in person. Everyone likes to hear happy news, and most senior leaders enjoy the opportunity to congratulate teams on successful projects. Providing this opportunity to those key stakeholders further strengthens those relationships you've been building all along. In today's globally interconnected environment, there's a strong likelihood that you will be working with all of these people again, so it's worth your time and energy to improve your ability to motivate and influence them in the future by recognizing their contributions now.

In addition to a team celebration, it's a good idea to individually recognize your teammates, especially those who were particularly instrumental to the project's overall success. There are several ways to do this, and which way you choose is primarily dependent on their manager and the organizational culture. The simplest, and probably most effective, way to recognize an individual is by sending a short note to the team member's manager expressing your appreciation for their contributions. Take care to highlight those contributions the manager will value most and be sure to copy your teammate on the note. Many organizations have formal recognition programs, and these are also a great way recognize the team. Finally, it's a nice touch to provide some specific feedback to your teammates' managers as they are collecting input for the yearly performance reviews. Note that if you want to do this, you will probably need to set a reminder in your own calendar lest you forget to take care of it when performance evaluation time comes around, since many organizations do this only once a year.

The last thing you need to do for your teammates is to release them from the project work. Here you are clearly declaring the project finished and letting them know that they can move on to focus on other work. In PM-centric organizations, there's usually a specific process or tool the PM needs to utilize to indicate that the project resources are now available for other work. However, not all organizations are so organized and this release happens informally. In those circumstances, simply send out the project summary, once again thanking the team for their hard work, and wish them good luck on their next project. It's also a nice gesture to offer to help out if they have challenges with their next project so that you keep that professional relationship going long after this project wraps up.

You've probably noticed that all of the discussion so far has been focused on the scenario where the project was successfully executed, but what about those instances where the work got done, but you can't really call it a success? Sometimes you close out a project knowing that it wasn't successful and the best you can do is call it done and move on. What do you do then? Well obviously, you're not going to throw a big party, and those glowing recommendations for departmental awards are out, but you still need to take care of your team. Even in the epic failure scenario, there are probably a few standout team members who deserve recognition, so be sure to send that note to their manager highlighting their contributions. In this kind of situation, as the team leader, it's incumbent upon you to help the team understand what went wrong and whether or not they could have prevented the downhill slide. You will need to own up to your failures as well. Did you pay enough attention to monitoring the project execution? Could you have spotted the slipping schedule, the increasing scope, and/or the additional risks sooner? Sadly, this is a common failure when projects derail, as they often could have been put back on the tracks if someone had recognized what was going on earlier. Finally, be sure to let your team know that despite how it turned out, you genuinely appreciate all of their hard work to get the project done. It may not have been the best project any of you will ever work on, but don't forget that you got the job done in the end, and that's worth something, isn't it?

YOU STILL FAILED

There's a weird scenario that you will likely encounter if the release did not go well. This is what happens: you're cleaning up the mess, you've let the team know that despite obstacles they did some good work, and you've wrapped things up on a high note, but now someone thinks that the team should be rewarded in some way. This is usually a manager, or one of the teammates, and it's tempting to fall into the trap of rewarding failure, so be careful. The fact of the matter is that the team failed. Sure, they may have snatched this one from the jaws of death, but the truth is that they should never have gotten within chomping distance of those jaws in the first place. I won't punish you for a failure if you learned something, but I sure as heck won't reward you . . . because you still failed! So what do you do when your manager sidles up to you and says something like this: *"So, Melanie, can you write up that division recognition for the project team since they finally got that new product out the door?"* Similarly, how do you respond when one of your teammates says, *"Now that we've completed the release, is there going to be a celebration lunch?"* Here's what you do: you lead with the data and say something like this: *"I'm not sure that that reward is warranted this time. We missed our commitment to deliver the product by 3 months/we ended up $50k over budget/the product doesn't meet the heat resistance threshold/etc., so while we did accomplish a lot, we didn't achieve the* *business need this project was supposed to fulfill. The good news is that we learned a lot and are well positioned to be successful on the next project. Let's knock that one outta the park and then we can celebrate.*" Everyone likes to get recognized and no one is sad when lunch is free, but it's not a good idea to get in the habit of rewarding failure or even mediocre performance. At its core, a reward is meant to motivate future behavior, so be sure that you're rewarding the behavior you want to see in the future. Last, understand that if every accomplishment is rewarded, regardless of difficulty or impact, then the overall value of this kind of recognition is devalued across the organization. Resist the temptation to reward failure, but be sure that you acknowledge the significant effort required to execute the project even if it was a failure.

Checklist #5—Closing the Project

It's interesting to me that even experienced project managers cut corners when it comes to the Closing Phase. You see, they get so distracted by the cool, flashy newness of their next project that they neglect to clean house between projects. This is sloppy and it creates problems down the road. Close out your projects all the way by conducting a retrospective, cleaning up after yourselves, publishing a summary of what the project team achieved, closing out with your key stakeholders, and taking care of your team.

The following checklist identifies the major tasks you need to complete as you and your team wrap up the project. Many of these items will be done simultaneously. Again, the important thing to keep in mind is that you should be doing all of these tasks; they represent the minimum tasks you need to perform during the closure process.

Checklist #5—Closing the Project

- ☐ Facilitate the project retrospective
- ☐ Clean house
- ☐   Appropriately disposition all project material (HW & SW)
- ☐   Post all collateral to their permanent locations
- ☐   Archive important project artifacts
- ☐ Publish project summary
- ☐ Obtain key stakeholder agreement that the project work is complete
- ☐ Hold a celebration for the team (if warranted)
- ☐ Recognize individual team members for their contributions (if warranted)
- ☐ Release resources from the project to be available for other work

---

That's it! You're done with the project. Take a few minutes to reflect back on the work you've done in the Initiating, Planning, Executing, and Closing Phases. I hope by now you deeply understand what I meant at the beginning when I stated that the hard part of project management is not mastering the mechanics of the job. I've walked you through the tasks and processes that are absolutely critical to successful project execution. They are not overly difficult or complicated to perform. You probably need a bit more practice in some areas, but you're well on your way to mastery. For your next project, you should be able to use the checklists provided to stay on track, and we will talk more about that in Chapter 9. Next up, I'm going to walk you through that minefield of a low project management maturity organization, where we will discuss just what you should do if you're managing projects in a truly Wild Wild West environment.

Reality Check
Applying the Mechanics in the Real World

It's not enough to understand how to execute a process or produce an artifact; you have to be able to do those things within the chaotic circus that is your real job, not that mythical "made-for–TV" job you wish you had. Now we move into that gray area between the best practices we've just discussed and what it takes to get the job done in the real world.

Chopping Down Your Project Mechanics

Now that you understand what solid project management looks like when the mechanics of the job—things like the schedule, risk management, and communications planning—are executed properly, it's tempting to believe that's the best way to manage any project. Okay, it really is, but let's not forget that projects are still executed in organizations where project management discipline is as ephemeral as dandelion fluff. What do you do if the mere words "Work Breakdown Structure" cause instant rebellion? How do you convince people to devote time to planning the project work when they are wild-eyed and twitchy, just chomping at the bit to get started on the "real work"? Let me teach you what experienced project managers already know: how to go into stealth mode!

Seasoned project managers know that there's more than one way to achieve their objectives, be it planning the project or orchestrating change control, and the key to their success is an accumulation of tools for performing the mechanics of project management. If you're just starting out, you should absolutely focus on learning how to develop these plans and tools as we've discussed. As you master your craft, you will encounter different tools and processes that will also work. Learn those techniques, building up your project management toolbox as you go. There will come a time in your career when you will be smack-dab in dandelion fluff territory, so it's best to be prepared.

© Melanie McBride 2016
M. McBride, *Project Management Basics*, DOI 10.1007/978-1-4842-2086-3_7

Stealth Mode

The first thing you need to understand when you're asked to lead a project in a low-PM-maturity organization is that your fancy, dancy project management words are gonna freak 'em out. People hear "Network Diagram" and think "busywork," because they're not like you ... they haven't read this book! Seriously, they don't understand the mechanics of building a realistic schedule, so all of this brainstorming and playing around with sticky notes just looks like a waste of time to them. Further, it's probable that they have had bad experiences with poorly developed schedules that only contributed ambiguity and frustration to a past failed project. They have project management baggage. You deal with this by simply not using works like "Network Diagram" and instead say something like this: *"Okay, now that we've got a good understanding of all of the work we need to do, let's lay it out on a timeline."* You basically convince them to do the work of creating the WBS and the Network Diagram without actually making a big deal of the process. See, I told you this was stealthy.

The other stealthy thing to do when confronted with mass resistance is to take care of some of the mechanics yourself and present them to the team as something you were fooling around with on the side. Here I'm talking about things like the Release Readiness Checklist. You can do a fair job of it by yourself during planning and simply bring up the items you think need to be addressed in an offhand manner. Try something like this: *"So, since these instructions are for our external customers, do we need to get Legal to buy off on them beforehand?"* Here's the really cool part about this approach: you look brilliant! It's likely that that Legal review would have slipped through the cracks in a low-PM-maturity organization and someone would have had a last-minute scramble to get it done before the release. By bringing up these due diligence items early, they are easily accepted as work that needs to be done, you get kudos for thinking of them, and the team has one less fire during the release process. You don't actually have to tell them that you created a specific checklist during planning, especially when you have reason to think that this will distract the team from the work at hand. You simply pull out the checklist a few weeks before release as something you pulled together to *"double-check that we're on track for the release in 2 weeks."*

What Project Management Processes Are Absolutely Necessary?

If you're going into stealth mode, then it helps to be very clear on what project management processes and artifacts are absolutely necessary, so let's talk about those now. In Chapters 2 through 6, I've repeatedly emphasized that those processes and artifacts discussed are the absolute minimum work you need to do to properly manage a project, but that assumes that you're working in an organization that is receptive to project management discipline. This is not always the case, and while you can be stealthy about executing these processes, it's good to understand which artifacts are critical to managing any project, in any environment. Think of this as project management triage.

In my opinion, the most critical artifact necessary for managing any project is the project schedule. I *always* build one. There are certainly times when that schedule isn't as detailed or as comprehensive as I'd prefer, but even a half-baked schedule is better than none at all. Think of it this way: you're the navigator for the team and you need to be able to give them directions on where to go. No, you can't tell them to go jump in a lake! You have to provide actionable directions with respect to the work and when it needs to be done. If no one is providing this information to the team, then they are essentially wandering around lost in the desert, constantly seduced by the mirage of a finish date. You can always create a schedule even in the most ambiguous of environments; it's just not always fun.

The most critical process for managing any project is executing the stakeholder management plan. The process of creating the stakeholder management plan is simple and provides invaluable insights to the project manager. The work to build these critical relationships will not be viewed as "work" in low project management maturity organizations, so you need to balance this relationship building with the perception that you're a social butterfly. The stronger your relationships with the key stakeholders are, the more likely it is that the project will be successful. Unfortunately, this area is fraught with soft skills challenges which we do not cover in this book. Once you master the mechanics of project management, then I strongly encourage you to focus on building your soft skills toolbox next. This work is something you can plan and execute by yourself, so don't cut this corner.

The last process I consider critical to any project is that of controlling changes. Here I'm not so worried about stopping changes, or the wild churn of scope that's common in low-PM-maturity organizations, as I am in ensuring that the team and stakeholders understand the impact of these changes. There will always be changes to the scope of work, the underlying assumptions, and the expected timeline, no matter the project environment. In organizations where the PM discipline is low, the rate of change and the magnitude of these changes are higher than in more mature organizations that are actively controlling the project pipeline. This is reality, so you need to be able to lead a team in that environment, and the only way to contain the madness is to set up a process for understanding the inevitable changes to the Triple Constraint. This is one piece of structured process that I insist on, and while I've had teams push back on a formal process, they all eventually see the value in a change control process by the time the project is done.

Now here's the cool part about stealthily introducing some project management discipline into a wild and crazy environment: you look like a rock star! All of a sudden, you come in as the project manager, and people know what to work on and when it needs to be done. Management gets clear and timely updates about the project work. There's a sense that this project is "under control," and you're the brilliant one who was able to wrangle that wild bunch of mustang developers. Obviously you can't solve big, systemic problems with just one project, but even a little of your mad PM skills will result in more successful, better-run projects, especially in a world where project management is viewed suspiciously as overhead. You build some credibility on that first project, which allows you to introduce more project management best practices in the next one, and eventually you find yourself leading project teams that execute smoothly and successfully every time. Sure, you probably can't fix an entire organization, but you can lead drama-free projects that allow your teammates to do their best work, and at the end of the day, isn't that what you are working toward?

Streamlining for Low-PM-Maturity Organizations

Going into stealth mode and focusing on only the most critical processes and artifacts will take you far in low-PM-maturity organizations. To go even further, you can deliberately streamline some of the project management mechanics we've discussed so far. Note that I'm not advocating stripping all of your project management skills down to the bone; rather, I'm suggesting that in organizations that do not understand the discipline necessary to effectively lead successful projects, there are some shortcuts you can take, so let's discuss those now.

The first thing to slash is the project charter. The sad truth is that many organizations barely pay lip service to this document, which PMI sees as the cornerstone of any project. If your organization doesn't even understand the concept of a charter, that's okay. The important thing to do is gather the information that the charter is supposed to convey. In Chapter 2, we covered this strategy in detail, so I won't repeat it here; just know that it's perfectly fine to ditch the charter as long as you make sure that the key stakeholders and the project team are all in alignment on the high-level Triple Constraints of the project.

There's a streamlined way to create a schedule in a highly ambiguous environment. Start with milestones and major work packages. Ask the team to help define those and tell them to be "conservative" on their estimates, stressing that you can always "optimize" the schedule later. Note that you want to use those specific words so that your team doesn't feel pressured to give you an unrealistically short estimates or freak out about the idea of pulling the schedule in. If you're in this situation, you may find it necessary to make some assumptions about major deliverables or receivables. Simply create a milestone where it makes the most sense, then spin the rest of the dates around it, moving that milestone to where it fits logically in the timeline as you and the team learn more about the workflow you need to execute. It's also a good idea to dial down the complexity of the schedule itself, so consider using a spreadsheet or even—gasp!—PowerPoint to build the schedule. The goal here is to create something that you and your team can use, so while a spreadsheet means more work for you, it may be the best choice for your team and the particular environment you find yourself in at the time.

As I mentioned, strong change control is essential, but you can also chop that process down to something realistic to execute in a low-PM-maturity environment as well. First, focus your attention on the project-level changes and create a simple change request form. This should include what the change is, why it's needed, and who is impacted. Make the intake process for this form painless by posting it in a common area and even going so far as to fill it out as a team when a change is introduced. Review this form as a team and capture the impact of the change by collecting the work estimate to implement (don't forget validation and documentation work!) and when the team expects it to be implemented. If the change affects anyone outside the team, then simply communicate the change plus its impact to them.

For program-level changes, sidestep the peer pressure by agreeing to look at the impact and report back. Once your team has evaluated the change, do that: report back. The key here is to give the program team data they can then use to make a decision about whether or not they want to go forward with the change. Even if your organization is really low on the ole PM maturity meter, it's important to report back the impact of any changes. Sure, this may not change the decision to execute the change, but you have a professional responsibility to make the implications of the change clear to the decision-makers. Later, when you're getting hammered for slipping the schedule, you can clearly articulate the amount of unplanned work the team took on as a result of these changes. It may not save you from the verbal harangue, but it will educate the decision-makers on the consequences of their decisions, and that impact analysis will likely be taken more seriously the next time.

The key to streamlining the risk management process is simplicity. Keep the initial meeting to identify, rate, and rank the risks short: no more than an hour. Dial down the tracking of the risk management plans by integrating those tasks into the project schedule so that the team doesn't have to update a separate file. Focus only on the top three to five risks that your team can actually affect. If you take care of the most likely risks that your team can prevent, then that's good enough. Oh, and it should be noted that you need to be careful about over-communicating your risk register, since the team can't honestly address all of the project risks they identified. It's not uncommon for key stakeholders to push you to manage all of the identified risks in organizations that aren't familiar with formal risk management. To these people, all of these risks sound scary, but they can't balance that fear with the reality of the available headcount.

Finally, don't forget to just downplay the formality of project management. If the organization doesn't have a gate review at the end of Planning, requiring approval to move into Execution, then don't make a big deal of that transition. Release planning is another area where you can downplay the mechanics of the task and get buy-in from your team. Instead of a 2-hour meeting to plan the release, bring up the topic in your weekly team meeting. Start the ball rolling with questions like *"what are the steps to the release process and who will execute each one?"* and *"do we need to request any additional lab space or special equipment for the release?"* You will find that your team is receptive to this advanced planning, especially if you don't make it feel like additional work to them. Simply integrate it into the normal team updates well ahead of the release and then go from there.

What to Do If There's No Formal Approval Process for Your Project Release

There is one area where you can't afford to streamline or cut corners, and that's with the approval to release the project deliverables. If you find yourself in an organization that doesn't have a defined process for approving releases, then you need to create one for your project. Similarly, if your organization's process is rather loose, then you need to formalize it. Over the years, I've found that senior leaders purely love to be the final approver, but they may not want to be held accountable for the results of those decisions. There's a whole pile of work in the field of psychology trying to explain why people behave that way, but for now, understand that this is what you may be up against. In these situations, you need to use a defined decision-making process complete with actual data and peer pressure.

To formalize a release approval decision, use the Go/No Go decision process we discussed in Chapter 6. Before the actual decision-making meeting, you need to explain the Go/No Go decision process that will be used and clarify who actually gets to make that decision with your key stakeholders. You should also meet individually with each decision-maker to review the project deliverables and the due diligence that the team has done prior to the actual decision meeting; addressing any concerns they may have before the Go/No Go meeting. At the start of the meeting, clearly articulate who the decision-recommenders are, who is affected by the decision, and who will actually make the decision. From there, follow the process outlined previously. The trick here is to subtly use peer pressure to get to a decision. After everyone has provided a recommendation, you put the decision-maker on the spot to actually do their job and approve (or disapprove) the release. You're basically stroking their ego when you emphasize their role as the bigwig decision-maker while applying peer pressure by having the team present and waiting for said decision. Infuse this meeting with gravitas and formality; project seriousness and professionalism yourself and the others will behave the same. Something interesting happens when you do this: people take this decision-making process more seriously. After a while, you won't even have to badger people to attend these meetings; the organizations' culture changes such that these meetings are required and important.

Not all organizations are at the same level of maturity when it comes to project management discipline, and you will eventually find yourself challenged to lead a team in a space that doesn't value project management. You can still be successful at the job, but you may need to tweak your mechanics and processes to best fit the environment. Remember that no matter the organization's culture or tolerance for project management shenanigans, you should always create a project schedule, actively manage stakeholder expectations, and manage changes to the Triple Constraint. As you gain experience, you will learn new and hopefully more efficient ways to perform the mechanics of project management. These ideas will inform your choices for how you go about managing projects in any environment, but they all start with a firm grounding in the basics, covered here in Chapters 2 through 6.

PMP-ing Your Project with Flashy Methodologies

In the previous chapter, we discussed specific strategies for leading projects in an environment that is unfamiliar or unsupportive of project management discipline. In that type of environment, you need to dial down the PM terminology and streamline processes. Now let's flip the coin and talk about the opposite side: some ways to go beyond the basic mechanics we've covered so far when you find yourself in a PM-friendly organization. Yes, my friend, this chapter is all about bringing some PMP skills to the table. If you're feeling pretty comfortable with the fundamental mechanics we've been discussing so far or if you find yourself awash in a sea of senior PMs and aren't quite sure how to stand out, then this chapter is for you. Here we will cover some easy-to-adopt strategies for taking your project management to the next level by integrating some advanced techniques, creating and leveraging metrics to help you better predict your team's performance, and starting to build a foundation

© Melanie McBride 2016
M. McBride, *Project Management Basics*, DOI 10.1007/978-1-4842-2086-3_8

of historical data that will become your treasure chest of knowledge later. You don't need to hold a PMP to employ these strategies. Heck, you don't even have to be that experienced to use them: and that's the point! Remember way back in Chapter 1, I told you that the mechanics of project management aren't that hard and that you can master them with a little effort? Well, the same goes for these next techniques; they are simple to implement and will significantly improve your project management effectiveness.

A Sprinkle of Agile, a Dash of TOC....How About a Hybrid Model?

Way back in Chapter 3, we discussed the most popular project management methodologies, but the one we trekked through, exploring all its secrets, was the Waterfall method. Certainly, the Theory of Constraints (TOC) and Agile methodologies are excellent methods for managing projects on their own, but that doesn't mean that you can't borrow a few tidbits from each to up your game. You don't need to be a seasoned project manager to pull this off if you're judicious about which bits and pieces you borrow, so let's talk about that now.

One tidbit from the Agile methodology that can be leveraged within a Waterfall lifecycle is the concept of a burndown chart. Here's the basic idea: the burndown chart is a running list of requirements that the team needs to implement. Think of it as a backlog or bin list of requirements that need to be estimated and prioritized. I find it particularly useful to use this technique while planning a complex project. New requirements get plunked into the backlog to be analyzed and incorporated into the evolving Network Diagram during Planning. Using this technique can help you keep track of new requirements as they are realized while keeping the team focused on the work of systematically gathering requirements. Once you get comfortable with the mechanics of building a WBS and a Network Diagram, you can push the envelope a little further. You can do a first pass at these to artifacts using larger work packages to build the schedule. Then, during the Execution Phase, you can use that backlog list to populate those larger work packages in the schedule, thereby providing a level of flexibility in arranging the workflow that Waterfall typically doesn't support. This technique is a simplified version of rolling wave planning, and it will provide your team with the ability to rapidly react and respond to a changing environment while maintaining that overall project schedule and associated customer commitments. Here you're mixing some of the goodness of Agile (flexibility to arrange the work to focus on what's most important) into the structure and predictability of Waterfall.

To leverage some of the goodness of TOC, you need only employ schedule buffers and change your mindset. If you will recall, there's a subtle difference between the Waterfall and the TOC methodologies. While employing the TOC methodology, the team focuses on the rate of schedule buffer consumption, not the completion of each individual work package. If you've built your project schedule as we discussed in Chapter 3, then you've already baked in these buffers. The mindset change is this: instead of focusing on the specific work package deliverables, you lead your team to focus on the buffer consumption. Some tasks will finish early, while others will take longer than planned, but as long as you've got buffer left in the schedule then the team remains on track. This technique delivers a significant advantage to the project manager by fundamentally changing the team dynamic. Your team will feel empowered to do their best work because you've provided them with a schedule safety net. What you find is that team members are less distracted by the possibility of unanticipated, show-stopping defects or more-complicated-than-expected designs, and are instead focused on the work at hand. You aren't sidestepping the need to drive to a specific completion date for each work package; you've just adjusted that completion date to include some accommodation for reality.

Your Newest Secret Weapon ... More Metrics!

This next technique a dead-simple extension of what you are already doing during the Execution Phase. In Chapter 4, we covered the minimum metrics you should be actively monitoring during the Execution Phase of your project, so now let's expand on that a bit to bring a whole other level to your game. If you're already tracking Earned Value (EV) metrics, then you are familiar with the Schedule Performance Index (SPI) and the Cost Performance Index (CPI). You can think of both of these metrics as a ratio of executed work/incurred cost versus what was planned to be executed/incurred at any point in time. They are very useful metrics, as you saw in Chapter 4, but there's a simple way to gain even more insight into your project performance. It's sufficient to be able to understand your EV metrics at any given point, but what you really need is the ability to comprehend the EV trends over time. To do this, you simply graph SPI and/or CPI versus time, and in fact, many scheduling software packages will do this for you automatically. EV metrics won't change much from week to week, so you may miss seeing a slow-moving decline in execution unless you are paying attention to the data trends. Remember, this trend is a reflection of how well your team is executing the project plan, so if you see 3 weeks of declining SPI, then it's definitely time to figure out what's slowing the team down. What you want to see is a mostly straight SPI/CPI line somewhere above the 0.9–0.85 level. (Figures 8-1 and 8-2) That straight line means that your team is executing the work at 85–90% of the rate that was planned for the work. That's pretty respectable performance, especially when you consider that your schedule already has some buffer baked in.

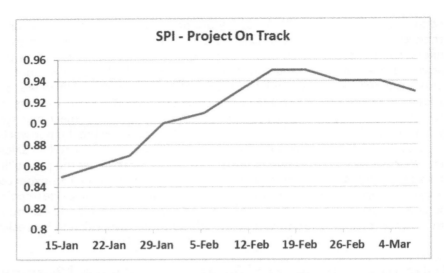

Figure 8-1. On track project SPI versus Time example. Note that while the SPI line is not perfectly straight, it remains well within the 90–100 band, which can be interpreted to mean that the team is executing at least 90% of the planned work on time

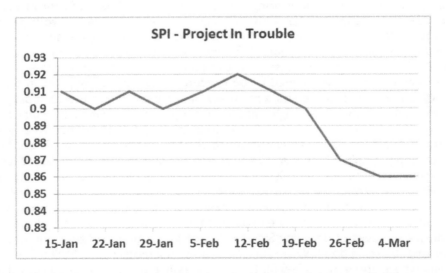

Figure 8-2. SPI versus Time example for a troubled project. Note that while the SPI remains within the 0.9–0.85 SPI band, the trend is clearly indicating that the team's ability to execute the work as planned is degrading. Immediate intervention is needed to keep this project on track

You can do the same thing with the percentage complete metric. Simply graph the percentage of the total work completed versus time. Here you should expect to see another straight line with increasing slope. (Figure 8-3) This indicates that the team is constantly making progress but that's all it tells you. What you don't want to see is a squiggly or flat line. If your trend line bounces around like a toddler in a bounce house, this indicates that there's a lot of churn in the scope of work and your team is executing a lot of unplanned work. (Figure 8-4) In that scenario, it's time to replan the project. If your trend flatlines, then this basically means that your team is no longer making progress. (Figure 8-5) This could mean that they are executing unplanned work, they hit a snag in the execution and the work is taking longer than expected, they simply lost focus on completing work packages, or everyone is on vacation. This graph doesn't tell you anything about how the team is performing relative to the baseline plan, because percentage complete is a pretty simplistic metric. However, the trend of percentage complete over time does give you some valuable insights that allow you to get in front of major problems early and course correct or replan as needed.

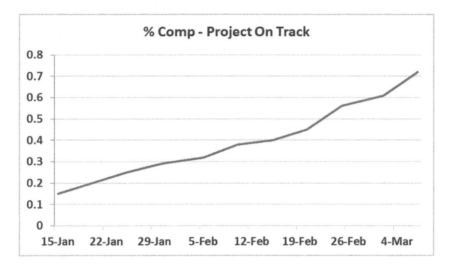

Figure 8-3. On-track project percentage complete (% Comp) vs. Time example. Note the steadily increasing slope of the % Comp line. This project team is consistently making progress; however, you cannot tell if the rate of work completed is aligned to that of the project plan

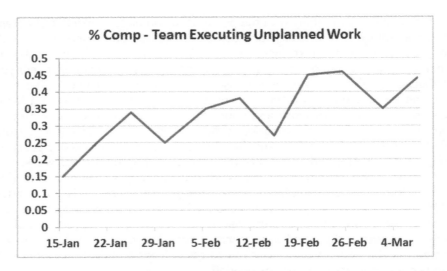

Figure 8-4. Excess unplanned project work % Comp vs. Time example. Note rapid swings in % Comp in this example. This project team is executing a significant amount of unplanned work. Immediate action is needed to get this project back on track, and it's likely that you will need to replan and recommit this phase of the project work. To do this update the WBS, the Network Diagram, and the schedule to incorporate this unplanned work

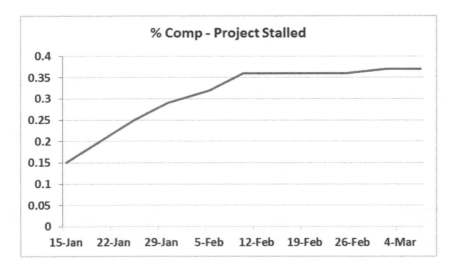

Figure 8-5. Stalled project work % Comp vs. Time example. Note the flatline behavior starting 12-Feb. This project team has stopped making progress and immediate action is needed to get this project back on track. Again, this graph does not comprehend the project plan, so it could be that no work has been planned for this timeframe. All the graph tells you is that work has essentially stopped

The thing is, most PMs don't dig this next level down when they are considering their EV or percentage complete metrics. Instead they pay lip service to the data while focusing on other things, all the while completely missing an easy opportunity to understand whether or not their projects are tracking to the baseline plan and customer commitments. These simple graphs tell you a lot about how your team is doing, take mere minutes to update, and will set you apart from your less focused peers, even if they have more experience.

Your Historical Data Treasure Chest

Data about how past projects performed is incredibly useful to project managers. It allows you to improve work estimates for new projects, it validates assumptions about how long certain work packages take to complete, and it can become the cornerstone of the scoping efforts for new projects. Most agree that historical data is important, but for many organizations, high-quality, relevant historical project performance data can be like the Holy Grail. Either the tools for collecting this information are too simplistic, yielding lots of data that is time-consuming to digest, or they are so complicated that real meaning is impossible to extract.

I hear it over and over again: *"I can't predict my team's future performance because we just don't have any usable historical data."* I'm sure that you don't have that historical data, but frankly that's a weak cop-out, especially if you've been managing projects in the same organization for a while. The truth is that there's a pretty small subset of this data that you need to dramatically improve your effectiveness, and you probably already have it on your laptop or PC. First, let's deep-dive into just what that subset of data is; then we'll figure out how to get it.

So, what data would be useful to you and your team during scoping? What historical data do you really need? First, you need data about how long past projects took to execute, a.k.a. their duration. Second, you need to understand a little about the scope of those projects so that you can extrapolate performance metrics of similar projects in the future. Third, it's useful to break down how long each phase of the project took. Fourth, it's very useful to understand how long major work packages took to execute. Honestly, if all you have are the first two pieces of data about enough past projects, you can do a lot of damage during scoping. If you can obtain all four data sets, you can dramatically improve estimation of effort and overall duration for future projects.

This list may seem overwhelming, but there's a dirty little secret I need to clue you into right about now: .almost all of that data is hidden in your e-mail archive! Yep, what you really need to do is just dive in, create a spreadsheet, and spend a couple of hours data mining your own e-mail. First, create a simple spreadsheet to collect your mining results. You will need some columns like "Project Name," "High-Level Scope," "Start Date," "End Date," and "Total Duration." Now start climbing through your e-mail to uncover that information for every project you've worked on in the past few years. Don't worry about how precise the dates are, because what you're really interested in is the total duration, and whether its 55 days or 60 doesn't matter that much. To obtain the "Total Duration," you merely count backwards from the finish date to the start date.

Once you've exhausted your own e-mail archive, you can also go look at archived project schedules that might help you further add to your growing list of past projects. These schedules can yield good data on how long each phase of the project took to execute and how long common work packages took as well. Once you've populated your spreadsheet initially, keep updating it every time you finish a project. It won't take too long before you do have that pool of good, relevant historical data to use during scoping and estimation. The trick really is to just block out some time and go find this data. If you're just starting out, well then just start off on the right foot by building that spreadsheet and collecting this information each time you complete a project.

If you really want to go for the gold, you need to understand how the execution of these projects went so that you and your team can do a better job with risk identification on future projects. This information is captured in the retrospectives for past projects. The challenge with this data set is that it's usually hard to extract usable information from these reports. Most organizations adopt key learnings either organically or through a formal, systematic process, so there's often not a lot of actionable items to be found by reviewing past project retrospectives. That said, if you and your team are tackling a new project that closely resembles a past one or is a further improvement on previous project, then it can't hurt to walk through those retrospectives as a team to see if there's anything useful to be found. Do this during a regular weekly team meeting in that "special topics" timeslot in the agenda. As you can see, this is pretty quick and it just might turn up some risks that need to be managed in your new project.

Find More Flashy Ideas

I've given you just a few easy ideas to increase your PM effectiveness, but don't stop there. You see, in the field of project management, there are always multiple ways to solve problems, and since the mechanics of the job are so straightforward, people are always coming up with tweaks and improvements. How do you tap into these new and improved techniques? One way to do this is to get involved in the PM community within your own company. Most large organizations have internal communities of practice focused on sharing project management knowledge. These folks hold regular meetings, publish newsletters, conduct training, etc., so all you need to do is tap into the information flow. Ironically, many senior PMs tend to ignore these forums or simply don't prioritize participation in these communities, so this is a great way to learn new tools and approaches that will differentiate yourself from some of your more experienced colleagues.

Another way to tap into new and improved techniques is to go hang out with your local PMI chapter. These professional organizations hold regular member meetings, coordinate training opportunities, and often host seminars and conferences. These events provide you with the unique opportunity to network with other PMs in a variety of industries and disciplines, so not only do you get exposed to new ideas, you also have the opportunity to build your professional network.

The widespread adoption of formal project management discipline means that there's a good chance you are, or soon will be, working in an organization with strong processes and controls to manage project work. In this chapter, we've discussed some pretty simple techniques you can use to increase your effectiveness as a project manager. I gave you some ideas about how to tweak the project lifecycle model to improve the team's ability to react to a dynamic environment. We also talked about a few simple metrics you can incorporate into your practice right now that will allow you to get ahead of potential problems that could derail your team's execution. By data mining your own e-mail, you can dig up a treasure chest of historical data that will make scoping your next project so much easier and more accurate. Finally, don't forget to participate in the various PM-centric communities around you. They are a great way to uncover fresh new ideas that will help you improve your game for your own projects. One thing all of these ideas have in common is that none of them are hard or time-consuming. In fact, it's the simple act of doing a little bit more than the next PM that will help you stand apart, lead more effective teams, and grow your skill set, especially when you're lost in a sea of much more experienced PMs.

Steering Your Project with Flexible Checklists

At this point, you should feel pretty comfortable with your understanding of the basic mechanics of project management, so let's talk a little bit about how to leverage the checklists you find at the end of Chapters 2–6. You can certainly use these checklists as they stand today to guide your work, but don't stop there! I'll give you some ideas on how to augment the content of the checklists to further improve your overall effectiveness, and we'll discuss some tips and tricks for managing multiple projects using these checklists. Think of them as a map and yourself as the wilderness guide for the project team. Your goal is to be able to figure out where to go or what to do next to ensure that the team is able to complete the work of the project, and these checklists will help you do just that.

© Melanie McBride 2016
M. McBride, *Project Management Basics*, DOI 10.1007/978-1-4842-2086-3_9

Using Checklists to Guide Your Work

The first thing to understand is that these checklists contain the essential elements needed to lead a project team to deliver the expected outcome. You really need to do all of them if you want to be successful. Trust me! I've come to understand the value of each element of these checklists the hard way, by either skipping them or doing them halfheartedly, and I've paid the piper. Every single time you skip one of these items you pay, and often you pay for the duration of that project. As an old college professor used to say, *"Pay me now, or pay me later."* For example, when I don't explicitly do risk management, I consistently see my teams consumed with firefighting even if it's only occasionally. This is wasted time and energy that the team could put to better use, but because we didn't come up with some basic risk management plans, we pay that piper.

You will also encounter bad advice from a boss or more experienced coworker. If they tell you that you really don't need to build a schedule because "the team already knows what to do," smile and nod ....then go off and get crankin' on that WBS. In case you're wondering, this actually happened to a colleague of mine! She went ahead and built the schedule because she honestly couldn't manage the project without one.

The beauty of using checklists is that they leverage the work and experience of someone else. In their book *Decisive: How to Make Better Choices in Life and Work* (Crown Business, 2013), Chip and Dan Heath (Chapter 4, page 79) talk about this idea of using checklists as a way to leverage someone else's work. Checklists contain someone else's solution to your problem. In short, by using these checklists you're reaping the benefit of someone else figuring out the best practices for managing projects. They are deliberately prescriptive, and if followed, keep you from forgetting an important artifact or process. In short, these checklists will keep you on track and give you the best shot at being effective as a project manager.

All of the checklists are collected together in Appendix A. **You can download them at this book's page on Apress.com (www.apress. com/9781484220856).** Print them out and hang them up where you can see them. Create a set of checklists for each project you manage. In short, integrate the process of checking each item off into your project management practice. Even the most experienced of us get distracted or lazy and forget to do some of these things, especially the easy ones! Utilize the checklists here to keep yourself on track every time, and soon you'll see dramatic improvements in your overall effectiveness as a project manager.

Augmenting the Checklists

These checklists represent PMI's best practices coupled with my own experience, but that doesn't mean you can't improve on them. I would caution you not to delete any item, but you can, and should, be adding to them as you gain more experience and understanding of what's required of you within your own organization. So, let's talk a bit more about what kinds of additions you can make to customize the checklists here for your practice.

Throughout this book, I've pointed out the nuances of working in an organization with a strong project management culture and ecosystem. These are the organizations with formal PMOs and good project management infrastructure. If you find yourself practicing in such an organization, then there's a good chance that you will need to augment your checklists with specific items. If you will recall, back in Chapter 3 we talked about figuring out any organizational requirements or required artifacts. These items were incorporated into the WBS and ultimately ended up in your project schedule. These are the kinds of things you want to add to your checklists. For example, often you will find that the gate review between Initiating and Planning requires a formal review and approval of the scoping results. In that instance, you will probably be required to fill out a form capturing the forecasted budget, resource requirements, deliverables, and a timeline. Add this form to your Initiating checklist. In short, update these checklists with any required processes or artifacts that your organization requires. This will help you remember to do them and avoid that late-night scramble to create the required artifact at the last minute.

You can, and should, do the same thing if you work in a less formal organization, but here the items you add to your checklist may be more, shall we say ...*nuanced*. In organizations with little or no formal project management infrastructure, I've found that you have to create some formality yourself for key deliverables. For instance, you really should have your key stakeholders and any decision-makers sign off on the proposed project budget, especially in a low-PM-maturity organization. This may mean that you hold a budget review meeting with the key stakeholders or that you meet with them individually, depending on the culture of your organization. Since no one is making you do this review, you need to add it to your Planning checklist to make sure that you don't forget this important step.

Further, there may be some "hidden" tasks that you unearth yourself that you don't want to forget to do for each project. Here I'm talking about things like making sure that you review the architecture with that highly influential but not formally involved stakeholder. You know, those key stakeholders that can tank your project, or make life very difficult for your team, even though they don't have any formal association with your project? You probably want to add a checklist item to the Planning checklist to ensure that those influential individuals are cool with the approach your team plans to take before exiting Planning. If you forget to do this task, then you and your team will have to negotiate that swamp of internal politics for the entire project because you didn't get this key stakeholder on board early enough.

It should be noted that if you're going to add these types of items to your checklist—and you absolutely should!—you need to word them in a generic way. Instead of a checklist item like *"Make sure that Melanie blesses the design before you exit Planning,"* use something like *"Review the design in the weekly Architecture Forum"* in the Planning checklist. If you call me out by name in your checklist, then you're implicitly giving me more power over your project's destiny than I probably should have. It's always better to have a generic checklist that you can share freely with your project team, your peers, and management.

Last, as you gain experience, you can add checklist items that are specific to your leadership style or that represent key learnings from past projects. For example, if you really got burned by a supplier that couldn't deliver to their commits, then perhaps you add a specific process around supplier selection to your Planning checklist. If you figure out a faster, more efficient way to ship material between sites, then you can augment your Execution checklist with that process as well. As you gain experience, you will learn new techniques and approaches that get the job done more efficiently or more effectively. By incorporating those learnings into your checklists, you continually improve your effectiveness.

The idea here is that the checklists you use should evolve over time to help you become more efficient and effective. By using these new and improved checklists, you don't have to stop and think each time: *"So how did we keep Melanie from endlessly nitpicking our design last time?"* You already know what the best practice is and when to execute it, because it's right there with a checkbox in front of it. One thing to note, however, is that you don't want to remove any of the core checklist items we've covered previously in Chapters 2–6. Keep in mind that these are the *absolute minimum* processes and artifacts you need to execute in order to lead a successful project. Augment the checklists as you refine your craft but don't lose sight of the core practices that are required to lead a successful project. It will be tempting to cut corners and ditch some of them as you gain some confidence, so when you do it—and you know that you will!—pay attention to what happens. My money's on the core checklist items. If you cut out the stakeholder management process once, I'll bet that you don't do it a second time because the results are so painful to deal with. So add to the checklist but don't cut any of the core items we've walked through.

Managing Multiple Projects with Checklists

Checklists really prove their value when you find yourself managing multiple projects simultaneously. When you find yourself in this situation, it can be difficult to keep track of where each project is in the lifecycle and which of the processes and artifacts you've executed for them. Here's where checklists will save your bacon. When you find yourself leading multiple projects, create a set of checklists for each and keep them in an accessible place. There will be meetings where you need to provide an off-the-cuff update, and by referring to your current checklist, you can easily skim it and give a respectable update. If you've got more than two projects to manage, or if your projects have similar work packages, then you need to go a step further to help keep them straight. Here's where I employ color-coding. I assign a specific color to each project then I add a small color-coded graphic to the header of each checklist. You can get fancy with that graphic, but honestly I just use a circle with the specific color fill. In this way, you can quickly see which project you're working on at that point. You can extend this color-coding to your calendar and note-taking to help center your brain on whichever project you're working on at any given time.

I've found that when I manage multiple, similar projects simultaneously, these checklists are the only way I can keep up and ensure that I don't drop any balls. In extreme cases, I've also created a quick chart in a spreadsheet with a stop-light (red, yellow, green) color-coding scheme to track each checklist item for each project. It's the only way I can keep all of that similar work straight, since it's so easy to mistake work done on one project for that done on another. So if you find yourself with several projects to manage, then do yourself a huge favor and create those color-coded checklists. Trust me, it will help immensely.

Utilizing checklists takes a lot of the ambiguity out of the work, since it's clear what you need to focus on next. There's plenty of basic project management instruction to be had out there, but that in itself is part of the problem. How do you know what to do next when you're bombarded with information? These checklists are there to help you navigate your way through any project, and the core items on them represent the essential best practices. You should be augmenting these core items with processes and artifacts your organization requires, and those that they don't require but you still need to do, and with those tips and tricks you learn as you grow your own project management capability. Further, these checklists are indispensable when managing multiple projects at once, especially if the work contents are similar. Print them out and hang them on your office wall. Share them with your PM colleagues. Following these checklists is the best way to ensure that you've covered all the bases and done due diligence in the management of your project.

Hitting the Open Road

We've gone through the mechanics of project management all the way from the flick of your key stakeholders' wrist, starting the project engine to Initiate the project, down through the valley of Planning and over the hills of Executing, drifting sideways through the Release and ending with a slick, skidding, parking-brake stop at Closing. Whew, what a rush! Okay, what that really means is that you've read through this book and are ready to tackle that next project, so again, where do you start? Once you're on that journey to focus on the mechanics of project management, how do you start immediately injecting some of the learning now without waiting until you kick off another project? Are there any road hazards you need to be watching out for? Further, let's inject a little reality here and talk about what you do when your project is a failure, shall we? Last, what's over that next rise, or in other words, where should you take your PM practice once you master the mechanics? Hold on, folks, those are the topics we'll be covering next.

Putting It in Drive, a.k.a. What to Do Next

Now that you know what good project management mechanics looks like, where do you start? The obvious and easiest answer is with your next project. Start that next project with Checklist #1—Initiating Phase in hand and meticulously check off each item. You will start by figuring out just what it is

© Melanie McBride 2016

M. McBride, *Project Management Basics*, DOI 10.1007/978-1-4842-2086-3_10

that your new project is supposed to achieve, any existing constraints, and who the major players are. Now, you honestly didn't need me to tell you that, did you? No, what you really want are some ideas and advice for integrating this focus on the mechanics into your in-flight projects.

There are a few of these practices and artifacts that you can integrate into your current project and realize some benefits right away, so let's talk about those now. Focused stakeholder management is a great place to start no matter where you are in the project lifecycle, and it's relatively easy to get started. Begin by building that stakeholder management tool we talked about in Chapter 2. Basically, you want to sit down and think about who the key stakeholders are, what they care about, and how they prefer to communicate. You probably already have a good feel for this if your project is already well into the Execution Phase. However, I'd bet my lunch money that you haven't really focused on actively managing those relationships yet, so now's as good a time as any to get started. Carve out an hour without distractions and go build that spreadsheet. Take it a step further and coordinate some regular meetings with those key stakeholders for the duration of the project. Simply by setting up regular synch-up sessions, you will go a long way to improving communication with those stakeholders; you'll start getting your arms around what their perception of the project work is and have opportunities to get in front of their concerns before they become show-stoppers. Remember that not all of these synch-ups will be formally scheduled with the other person, so don't forget to put placeholders on your calendar to remind you to meet up with your stakeholders informally. Oh, and since you were smart and calendared these sessions out through the life of the project, you won't forget about them and find yourself at the Go/No Go meeting with no idea how the decision will go.

Another bit of mechanics you can insert midstream is change control. In Chapter 2 we discussed what you need to do to set up your team for a Change Control Board, but that doesn't mean that you can't institute one anytime during Execution. If you find that the scope of work for the project morphs around like a psychedelic kaleidoscope, then putting some discipline in place to communicate and control changes is a very good idea. If you're attempting to add a new process to an already chaotic project environment, you want to lead with the value proposition. Go with something like this: "*Folks, since the scope of work seems to be pretty dynamic right now, I'd like us to start tracking these changes more formally so that everyone knows what's changing and what the plan of record is at any given time.*"

Here the value to the team is improved communication about what they should be working on right now, but the value-add to the project manager is a process for assessing these changes and comprehending their impact to customer commitments. By formalizing this process, you can start to control the rate of change and you will definitely improve communication across the team and possibly the program your project supports. The key to winning your team over to a more formal process is to make it easy to follow, so don't make the change request form too complicated and steer the focus of any discussion of the change away from the process and toward understanding the potential impact.

Unless you're going into a major replan and are going to recommit the project deliverables, it doesn't make sense to do a major overhaul of your project schedule. If you've already got a mess on your hands, that is, the schedule doesn't model reality enough to be predictive of the actual project work, then your best bet is to do some triage and muddle through as you have been doing. You and your team should attempt to identify missing work packages, but the problem becomes what to do about them. In many organizations, there's little appetite for pushing out the project release date, so you have to cut the scope of work or get additional resources. Realize that if the gap between reality and what you've already committed is significant, then you have a professional responsibility to notify your stakeholders. It won't be fun but you still have to do your job. If you do find yourself in a replan situation, then build the WBS and the Network Diagram. It may be necessary to start fresh and build a new schedule from the Network Diagram altogether if your current one is beyond saving.

There Will Be Bumps in the Road

Okay, I'd be remiss if I didn't talk about what you do when your project is a failure. It happens to the best of us and even if you've done your best to execute the mechanics properly, something could go horribly wrong. Often, what's gone wrong could have been prevented by solid mechanics and execution, but remember, we're still dealing with people who are the real wild cards in project management. When you deliver a Titanic of a project, you need to step back and reassess the effectiveness of your management of the project. This is a personal exercise and it requires you to look at the outcome and objectively understand what could have prevented the failure. To help you out, see Table 10-1 for some common root causes of poor project execution that can be directly linked back to the mechanics.

Table 10-1. Common Root Causes of Project Failure Linked to Poor Execution of the Project Management Mechanics

Failure Characteristics	Breakdown in the PM Mechanics
Schedule slips due to significant amount of unplanned work	Incomplete or missing WBS
	Incomplete or missing Network Diagram
	No explicit buffers included in the schedule
	Poor change control process
Significant amount of firefighting	Inadequate risk management (risk identification, response plans, tracking)
Final deliverable wasn't what was expected	Poor stakeholder management
	Inadequate requirements gathering
	Insufficient change control
Surprise "No Go" decision	Insufficient stakeholder management
"No Go" decision due to a failure to meet compliance requirements (legal, regulatory, privacy, etc.)	Inadequate release readiness planning
Late realization that the team cannot deliver on time	Weak or insufficient schedule
	Inadequate monitoring of project performance metrics
	Insufficient change control

As you can see, a whole lotta pain and suffering can be avoided simply by mastering the mechanics of project management. This is exactly why you need to focus on these simple, foundational processes and practices. By honestly evaluating what went wrong on a failing project, you can pinpoint areas to focus on next time. Once you understand that your projects are missing commits because the team isn't doing a good-enough job identifying all of the work involved up front in Planning, you can start focusing on building the WBS. This one simple task can alleviate most of your sources of slipping project schedules. It really is that simple. As I've said multiple times throughout this book, it's not the mechanics that are the hard part of project management, so sharpen your skills on them to allow you more time to focus on the truly challenging part; dealing with the people.

Watch Out for Those Hairpin Curves and Steep Inclines

Exiting the Planning Phase with a strong project plan isn't a total guarantee that your project will be successful, but it's a good start. The Real World isn't that predictable and you will find yourself faced with dramatic changes in the scope of work or unexpected reductions in resources from time to time. Back in the dark days of the Dotcom Bust, I found myself having to deal with unexpectedly cancelled project regularly; today I often find myself figuring out how to add some bit of capability to enable a radically new market or highly influential new customer. Sometimes the economy goes bust, or your customers come from somewhere else, or you figure out that the solution you found doesn't fit the problem you need to solve right now. That's reality, and project managers need to be able to adapt to these unexpected curves and deceleration of their projects.

The good news here is that if you've got well-developed project artifacts and the team is executing in a controlled manner, then adjusting to these changing road conditions is much easier. When your boss pulls you aside and says, *"Melanie, I need to know how quickly we can shut this project down and what it could save in projected spending . . . and I need it tomorrow,"* you've already got the tools to pull together some options for ramping down the project work. You make a copy of your project schedule and do "what-if" modeling to identify options for your boss. You can look at your risk register and be able to articulate what risks the company can avoid (or not) by shutting this project down. If you're tracking spending, then you can roll that information into the analysis as well. To be sure, this kind of analysis is no fun to do, but having the tools available to do it quickly and accurately does make it easier. Likewise, if your boss pulls you aside and asks what it would take to add a new feature to enable a new, adjacent market, you've got the tools to do that analysis as well. The key thing here is that this analysis is data-based and will provide your boss with the kind of factual information she needs to make some critical decisions, and really, those aren't the kinds of decisions you want made without real data.

The ability to adapt quickly to dynamic environment is just one of the reasons why it's important to follow these basic processes and generate the project artifacts outlined by the checklists in this book. Today's project teams need that adaptability to be able to quickly capitalize on the changes in their environment. Effective project management, having a strong foundation based on solid planning and processes, enables that adaptability by maximizing the amount of time your team can spend on the work that delivers actual value to the company and its customers.

Beyond the Mechanics

Once you feel like you've got a firm hand on the wheel with respect to these foundational processes and artifacts, what should you focus on next? Well you could continue down the path of refining and building your tool kit for the mechanics of the job. However, I think you'll get more effective at managing projects if you focus on building your soft skills next. So what exactly do I mean by "soft skills"? Let me break it down for you. Soft skills are things like communication and influence; they represent those intangible abilities that every leader needs to master to be effective and revolve around interpersonal communication.

Project managers need to get work done through other people, and to do that you need to be able to communicate the work that needs to be done, motivate others to perform that work, and influence them to do it better, faster, and with fewer resources. Sure, you can simply use a dictatorial approach to working with others, and that coupled with positional power will get some work done, but it's not sustainable. To lead team after team to successfully complete work, any leader needs to be able to connect with their teams to understand how to enable them. You can't get that information by simply standing around yelling at them.

The problem with soft skills of course is that these terms are vague and how you improve any given skill is deeply personal. If I tell you that you need to go focus on improving your influence skills, do you know what to do? Nope! We need a little more here to get started on our journey, right? We need to drill down a bit to get to some actionable ideas for how to improve your soft skills. There are a handful of areas that are particularly useful for project managers, so here's where we will focus: communication styles, empathy, difficult conversations, and holding others accountable.

Understanding Communication Styles

If you got feedback on your last performance review that you need to improve your communication skills, understanding the four communication styles should be your first stop. The idea here is that we all have a default communication style that we employ and even if we can move between the four styles comfortably we always return to that default style under stress. If you've come across this concept before, the names may sound slightly different to you but the idea is the same. Here are the four communication styles:

- Amiable—relationship-driven communicator; values feelings and inclusion above completing the task at hand; excellent team player and connector; open/approachable body language

- Analytical—data-driven communicator; values data over emotion; can appear cold and uninterested in personal connection; focused on the details

- Driver—achievement-oriented communicator; values progress and control over personal connection; does not like to be surprised; gets frustrated when others aren't moving "fast enough"

- Expressive—animated communicator; values the "big picture" over the details; often uses big hand gestures; provides plenty of non-verbal feedback

Based on these brief descriptions, can you tell which one you are? You may exhibit a combination of some of these styles, but you will definitely have one specific default. The point I want you to walk away with is that these communication styles are intrinsic to each of us and we can no more turn them off than we can change the length of our toes. What you can do is learn to recognize others' communication styles and then morph your own to mirror theirs.

Let me give you an example of what I'm talking about. You may be able to tell by my writing that I fall into the Expressive communication camp, so I'm all about telling a good story, waving my hands while I do it, and glossing over those pesky details. Many years ago I had an Analytical communicator for a second-level manager and had to deliver a project status update every week. Week after week these updates did not go well, and I could tell that this person thought I was a bubblehead with no clue what was going on with my project. During this time, I was introduced to this concept of communication styles and the idea that you can change your own style to improve communication. Being extremely frustrated and having nothing left to lose, I decided to give this idea of manipulating my own communication style a try. Imagine my surprise when it worked!

Here's what happened. I sent the project status to him so that he could consume the data before our meeting. During the meeting I forced myself to stick to the facts and I sat on my hands. I literally sat on my hands to keep from waving them around and to remind myself to stay focused on the data. The results were immediate and shocking. I could tell right away that we were actually having a productive discussion about the project and that I did not come across as a bubblehead. The second time I deliberately mirrored the Analytical's communication style, I was told that he was glad to see that I'd "turned the project around." As any PM will tell you, the project status doesn't change that much from week to week, so the data I was sharing hadn't changed but this person's perception of the work had, all because I'd changed my communication style to better interact with him.

Over the years, I've seen this play out over and over again. This ability to morph your own communication style to improve communication is a game-changer, and you will see your overall effectiveness at dealing with so-called "difficult" people dramatically improve. Now think about someone you have trouble getting along with. What is their default style? No, lying weasel does not count! The next time you have to interact with this person, try changing your style to match theirs and see how it goes. I'd bet my lunch money that you will be impressed by the results. To help you get started with this, Table 10-2 contains some suggestions for how you can adapt to the various communication styles:

Table 10-2. Ideas for How to Adjust Your Own Style to Improve Communication with Someone Else

Their Communication Style	How to Morph Your Own
Analytical	Send data ahead of time for them to review
	Focus the communication on the data
Driver	Project a sense of urgency and a commitment to the task
	Be direct and succinct in your word choices
Amiable	Start the conversation with some social chit-chat to build connection
	Focus on the impact to others
Expressive	Focus the discussion on the "big picture"
	Provide details and backup data offline

This technique is so powerful that I always start anyone who would like me to mentor them off on it. They create a list of everyone who is involved with their project and then they identify each person's communication style. We then brainstorm ways to improve communication with each person based on their style. Over time, as you focus on identifying other's styles and then adjusting your own, you will find that this becomes second nature; that is, you just don't have to think about it or sit on your hands. The other thing you will find is that the number of "difficult" people you have to deal with magically diminishes. Oh, they don't go away, to be sure; you just get better at communicating with them.

Build Your Empathy

Now let's switch gears and talk about empathy. The ability to empathize with others will help you tremendously as you work to improve your ability to influence and lead. The ability to understand another person's position from their perspective is called empathy. This is not the same thing as sympathy, which is the ability to feel pity or sorrow for another's situation. This is a subtle but important difference. This technique of putting yourself in someone else's shoes to understand what's going on behind the scenes helps you understand how to motivate and influence them. If you are trying to figure out how to influence me to complete those assembly instructions on time, you need to figure out why I'm slacking. You can take the empathetic approach with something like this: *"Melanie, I get it that you have three other projects of higher priority than mine, but we still need to get those assembly instructions done. How can we do that?"* Or you can go with the sympathetic approach this way: *"Melanie, I'm so, so sorry that you have so much work, but we still need to get those assembly instructions done. How can we do that?"* Now if you're me, which appeal is more likely to result in some realistic suggestions for how to get those assembly instructions done? The empathetic approach, right?

The trick to strengthening your ability to empathize with others is this: always assume that your coworkers have the best intentions and believe they are doing the right thing from their perspective. I honestly believe that none of my teammates come to work every day hatching evil plots to thwart me or derail my projects. Therefore, something else has to be behind that late bug or poor-quality deliverable, and this is where empathy comes in.

Let me give you a real-world example of what I'm talking about here. I lead a lot of product development projects, and every once in a while a team will find a major defect late in the test cycle or even during the release activities. Inevitably, when that happens, the question *"Why wasn't this caught in validation?"* comes up. It's like a knee-jerk reaction by engineering managers. If you believe that those validation engineers are doing their best with the best intentions, then you can start to figure out the real root cause of that defect. It could be that there were missing or vague requirements, there could be valid engineering reasons why it wasn't found, and of course it could be that someone dropped a ball somewhere. The point is that if you can put yourself in the shoes of that beleaguered validation engineer and try to see the situation from their point of view, then you will have deeper insight into what could have gone wrong. Further, by expressing that empathy you reinforce a collaborative team dynamic and help the team focus on solving the actual problem. All too often, those situations devolve into a witch-hunt for the "guilty" party, who presumable will be punished in some fashion, but all that really does is distract the team from solving the problem at hand, that critical defect.

Having Difficult Conversations

Improving your ability to have difficult conversations with stakeholders is another way to get some major bang for your buck while working to improve your soft skills. Many people avoid having conversations that they know will turn into unpleasant confrontations and do it without even realizing it. No one believes that they actively avoid confrontation, but it's human nature to avoid situations where we feel threatened. So how do you know if this is something you should work on? It's not really a question of whether you should work on improving your ability to have these conversations, but rather of when you can squeeze in the time to learn how to do them properly.

Think back to your last failed project. Would the outcome have been different if you'd directly addressed the fact that the team could not pull in the schedule without sacrificing scope or increasing resources? Did you walk away from a difficult conversation saying something like *"we'll just have to make it happen"*? Trust me, there's not a PM on the planet who hasn't had a similar experience, so now let's discuss how to deal with these challenging conversations differently.

The first thing you need to understand about difficult conversations is that you don't go into them cold. You have to do some prep work ahead of time. Well before the confrontation, find some time and a place where you can think to prepare. First, you need to understand what problem you are trying to address with this conversation. It helps to write this down, so type up, or scribble down, a succinct sentence that describes the problem you want to deal with. Next, figure out what points you need to make in this upcoming discussion. Again, the discipline of capturing your thoughts in succinct sentences really helps clarify your thinking. Then put yourself in the other person's shoes and think about the problem from their point of view. Yeah, it's that empathy thing again. If you believe that they are doing the "right" thing from their perspective, then what's motivating that behavior? How is their perspective different from yours? What are the key points they care about with respect to this problem?

Now go review and refine your problem statement and the points you want to make based on your insights into the other person's perspective. Last, dig up any supporting data you will need to define the problem and reinforce the points you want to make. Impartial data can often make the gravity of the issue to be addressed clear without resorting to blame or accusation. For instance, if you want to address the issue of my continually missing your weekly project team meetings, then simply stating that I've missed eight of the last ten meetings is pretty self-explanatory, so there's no need to open with the accusatory *"Melanie, you keep missing my project meetings!"*

How you conduct that difficult discussion is as important as the preparation work. If you are initiating the conversation, then the first thing you need to do is establish a sense of safety for the other person. Do this by choosing a neutral place to hold the discussion and by projecting a calm demeanor and explaining that the purpose of the meeting is to resolve the problem. You need to maintain your professionalism; do not detour into accusation. Most of the time, if you approach this conversation calmly from a problem-solving position, the other person will respond in a similar manner. If you've set up a meeting to discuss the problem, then understand that who you invite to the meeting can greatly influence how the other person reacts. If you've invited my boss to this meeting to discuss why I'm not attending your weekly team meetings, then you should understand that that fact alone will automatically put me on the defensive, and I definitely won't feel safe discussing the problem. You'd be much better off to attempt this discussion with me alone first.

If during this discussion I become this angry defensive hot mess, it's important for you to remain professional. Don't let the other person's drama suck you into behaving badly, as that only escalates the drama and blocks any kind of progress toward resolving the problem. Finally, wrap up the discussion by restating any agreements, or failures to agree, so that the other person is clear where the resolution stands. If you feel that this problem has not been resolved, then also be very clear about your next steps. It's completely okay to say something like this: *"Okay, Melanie, clearly we can't agree on the importance of your attendance in the weekly project meetings. I still believe that it is important for you to be there due to the critical role you play on the project. Therefore, I want you to understand that my next step will be to discuss this issue with your manager."* Don't throw that *"I'm gonna go talk to your manager"* card out there as a threat; instead, treat it as a professional courtesy to let them know what your next steps will be.

Okay, now what do you do about those difficult conversations you get sucked into? First, if you think there's a possibility of a meeting veering off into a difficult discussion, do the prep work we discussed ahead of time. In all honestly, there are should be very few surprise difficult conversations if you're actively managing your stakeholder's expectations. If you do get blindsided by such a conversation, remember to remain calm and use your professional voice. Stay away from accusation and pay attention to your own emotional reaction. If the other person is deep into the drama of the situation, try to re-establish a sense of safety or empathy. Try to understand what is really driving their anger and or frustration.

This is the time to do more listening than talking, so be sure that when you do talk your statements are factual and delivered with neutral emotion. In the example of my inability to attend your meetings, if you were to angrily confront the issue with me, I should respond with something like *"I completely understand your frustration with my lack of attendance. What I'd like you to understand is that I haven't been attending your meetings because they conflict with those of another, higher priority project."* This statement delivered in a calm, neutral tone can de-escalate the conversation while acknowledging the legitimacy of your frustration. The key to success in these situations is to remain in control of your own emotions and to not get sucked into the other person's drama. This, however, is very difficult to do, especially when the other person is locked into their own emotional response. If the conversation gets to the point where it's not productive or it becomes abusive, then it's time to disengage.

There are plenty of suggestions for how to disengage, but over the years I've found that the best way to do this is to calmly restate my position, acknowledge that we are at a stalemate, advise the other parties that I need to leave the conversation, and then physically disengage from the conversation. All too often people continue to justify their position when they've reached a stalemate, but this only serves to convince the other party that if they can just find a hole in your logic, then you will agree. At some point neither party can agree or come to a collaborative solution; that's when it's best to simply state your position and disengage.

Holding Others Accountable

The ability to effectively hold others accountable to the commitments they make is a tricky one to master. Most people think they are pretty good at this, but the reality is that we aren't. You see, holding someone accountable requires us to have those difficult conversations when our colleague fails to meet their commitments, and this is definitely one area where there's a tendency to avoid that confrontation altogether. However, to be effective as a project manager you definitely need to master this soft skill.

The first thing you need to understand is the two factors at play here: ability and motivation. To be able to effectively hold someone accountable, you must first establish ability. You will get nowhere fast if you're trying to hold me accountable to complete a task I have no clue how to execute. Similarly, if I think I know how to do the job but I don't understand the work involved, then again, holding me to a completion date is fruitless. Therefore, the first thing you need to do when you identify a teammate who is falling behind on a deliverable is to establish that they have the ability to complete the task. This sounds simplistic, but trust me, there's a lot more going on under the hood.

A good bit of the time, when I'm trying to figure out why someone is late with a deliverable, the root cause is related to ability. Either they are waiting on a deliverable themselves, they don't really know how to execute the work and don't feel comfortable admitting it, they are executing the work in an overly complicated way, they don't have the tools or training they need to do the work, or they haven't managed their time such that they can get the work done on time. Trying to get someone to meet a commitment when they don't have the ability to do so is the equivalent of beating your head against the wall; all you end up with is a headache. You must establish that the other person has the ability to do the work before you can hold them accountable.

The second factor you need to address is the other person's motivation, and this is where it gets hard. When we talk about holding someone accountable, what we are really talking about is influencing them to complete a task. To influence this person, you need to understand their motivation and then go attempt to increase their willingness to complete the work. Remember, you want this person to actually complete the task, so you have to deal with their motivation to complete it. If you haven't done so already, then you need to have an actual conversation with this person and try to understand what's really going on. Are they distracted by other assignments? Do they feel valued and listened to? Do they really comprehend why this work is important not just to themselves but to the organization? Are they dealing with tough personal issues? Once you understand what's motivating their current behavior, then you can take steps to influence a change. You can empathize with their situation, revamp the task, provide context to help them understand why this work is important, help them see the consequences of their actions (loss of trust, increased work for teammates, etc.), and you can explain the consequences of failing to meet the commitment, all with the goal of increasing their motivation to complete the task.

Once you've established ability and done what you could to affect motivation, it's time to get down to the business of holding them accountable. Right out of the gate, you need to confirm that both of you have the same understanding of what was committed. Often, there's a fundamental communication breakdown here and you are not on the same page as to what was committed. At this point, you may need to accept a new commitment to get the work done. Whenever you are discussing an important commitment with a colleague, establish a follow-up session with clear expectations. By formalizing the follow-up, you are emphasizing the importance of the deliverable and signaling to the other person that you are paying attention to their work. If the other person doesn't meet this revised commitment, then it's time for that difficult conversation.

You should be very clear about the consequences of this missed commitment, and these things are not necessarily tangible. While I may be very aware of the impact to the project if I fail to deliver, what I'm probably missing is the impact to my professional reputation. A good PM will make sure that I understand those implications well before I miss the commit, and they will work with me to either recommit or provide some additional resources, if the work turns out to be more difficult that expected.

When you are trying to hold others accountable, it's imperative that you not lose sight of the real goal, which is to complete the work. Accountability should not be synonymous with punishment, nor should it be done after the commitment is missed. This needs to be an ongoing process; an integral part of monitoring the progress of the project work. What you're striving for is a team dynamic where issues are raised early and commitments aren't missed because they are adjusted in real time as needed. You can't get your team to that state if you're constantly using accountability as a club to beat them into submission.

Let me be clear here: I'm not advocating that you ignore a poor performer nor am I suggesting that there's really no negative consequence to missed commitments. What I am saying is that you should be overseeing the work in such a way that everyone on the team feels accountable to complete their work, and that means that you need to step in and help your teammates figure out what's blocking their progress from time to time. If you find yourself having to deliver negative consequences for a missed commit, then you should understand that at some level you failed to influence this person to complete their work on time. Perhaps this slacker really is a lyin' weasel and you did all that you could to turn the situation around before having to drop the hammer down on them. That's okay, because sometimes that's your reality; just be sure to take some time to think about what you could have done differently and understand what you would do differently next time. See, I told you this was tricky stuff!

In this chapter, I've tried to give you some ideas for where to take your project management practice next. I firmly believe that by taking the time to master those foundational processes and artifacts of the job will dramatically improve your effectiveness as a PM. Once you're comfortable with the mechanics of the job, it's time to start improving your soft skills. If you'd like to learn more or need some ideas on where to go next, please see Appendix D for a list of additional resources for improving your soft skills.

The End of the Road

We come now to the end of this particular road, and I truly hope that you're able to see the light at the end of the project management tunnel now. When you're new to this game it's easy to be overwhelmed with the amount of information out there and it's hard to figure out where to start. Throughout this book I've preached a basic concept: *the quickest way to improve your project management efficiency is to focus on the mechanics of project management.* Mastering these foundational processes will absolutely improve your skills and your confidence, resulting in increased effectiveness as a project manager. This does take some focused effort on your part but the return on your time is immediately realized. People are often confused about what it is that makes project management so hard. It's not the actual work of planning a project, for instance; it's the soft skills needed to get all of your stakeholders on the same page that's hard. Once you've figured out these foundational processes and how to do them, you'll have more time to devote to leading your team and managing your stakeholders.

To start our tutorial on the mechanics of project management, we broke down the project lifecycle by phase and identified the specific mechanics that apply. In Chapter 2, we talked about how to figure out what you're supposed to deliver, with or without a charter, and we started building the tools to manage your stakeholder's expectations. Then we moved on to the meat of the work in Chapter 3, where we discussed all of the processes and artifacts that make up the project plan. Here we delved into the systematic process for developing a schedule to ensure that all of the project work is captured and that the overall timeline is realistic, balancing the elements of the Triple Constraint.

© Melanie McBride 2016
M. McBride, *Project Management Basics*, DOI 10.1007/978-1-4842-2086-3_11

Next, we moved on to executing the project in Chapter 4, and here we discussed how to monitor the progression of work and to take actions to get the work back on track as needed. In Chapter 5, we talked about that special subset of the Execution work, the release process. To wrap things up, we covered closing the project in Chapter 6; it should be noted that the Closing processes are pretty simple to execute, so don't forget about them.

Moving on, beyond the mechanics of project management, we ventured into reality. Because you don't work in a perfect world where every PM is lauded and the management chain showers your project with resources, you need some help figuring out how to integrate these basic processes into your actual work. In Chapter 7, I provided some ideas for how to adjust if you're leading projects in an organization that perhaps doesn't value project management as much as it should. Here we talked about how to streamline the mechanics even more and how to inject some formal accountability into the release process. In Chapter 8, we flipped the coin and talked about some more advanced, yet still simple, techniques you can bring to bear when you find yourself working in a sophisticated project management shop. These ideas will help you stand out when you find yourself swimming with the PM sharks to set yourself apart from your peers. Chapter 9 provided a quick tutorial on how to use the checklists you find here and how to evolve them as your practice matures. Finally, in Chapter 10, we wrapped it up with a discussion of what the heck you actually do next. Here we covered some ideas for integrating the mechanics right into your in-flight projects, and we connected some of the common project failure modes with specific processes so that you can focus your continuous improvement energy where it's needed most. We also dipped a toe into the roiling waters of mastering soft skills, with some suggestions for where to take your improvement efforts next.

Beyond improving your effectiveness by mastering the mechanics of the job, there's a side benefit that you shouldn't overlook. If you've got the mechanics down cold, you will find these skills are your secret weapon when it comes to building credibility. By mastering the processes necessary to plan a project and integrating the monitoring and control mindset, every project you lead will execute more predictably. When you commit to deliver that new web portal by the end of July, guess what? The chances of that happening on time dramatically improve as your project management competency improves, and this is *independent* of the environment the project team has to live in. Each time you meet a project release commit, your credibility improves, because while executing successfully is important, I'd argue that executing predictably is much more important. Believe it or not, your management chain does know that not every project is going to be a home run, so what they really value is the predictability of the project execution. Most of the time, your project is part of a bigger initiative, and delivering when you say you will allows others to better plan and execute their own work. To be clear, it's very important to deliver successful projects, but you don't want to lose sight of the bigger picture either, and you need to understand that delivering predictably is what matters the most.

Along with greatly improving the predictability of your project releases, mastery of the PM mechanics also helps you look like a rock star when it's time to change jobs. Project management is a highly transferable skill set that spans all major industries and whose mechanics are industry/disciple independent. This means that when you're ready to branch out into a new field or just a new organization, having these project management mechanics in your back pocket can make all the difference. Personally, I've successfully changed fields and engineering disciplines, and I've switched from highly technical organizations to more operationally focused teams mostly because I'm good at the mechanics of the job. What I've found is that since I already know the steps and processes necessary to properly plan for a project, I can focus my energies on building relationships with key stakeholders, developing a collaborative team dynamic, and spinning up on this new area. There's no way I could have made even one of those job jumps if I hadn't first mastered the mechanics of managing projects; the learning curve of a new organization would have been too much to overcome if I was still struggling with how to build a comprehensive project schedule.

Altogether, this body of work should set any new project manager off on the right foot, and it will help junior project managers improve their effectiveness with straightforward instructions and advice to fill in any gaps they may have in their project management knowledge. Good luck out there!

Appendix A: Project Management Checklists

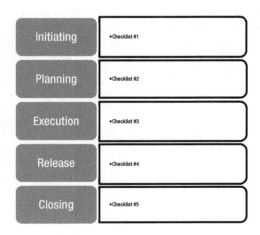

Initiating	• Checklist #1
Planning	• Checklist #2
Execution	• Checklist #3
Release	• Checklist #4
Closing	• Checklist #5

© Melanie McBride 2016

M. McBride, *Project Management Basics*, DOI 10.1007/978-1-4842-2086-3_12

Checklist #1—Initiating Phase

The Initiating Phase of the project is where it all starts. Key information is gathered, scoping is performed, and the project kick-off meeting is conducted. Complete these major tasks and you are ready to enter the project's Planning Phase. These items are arranged in chronological order, but note that you may end up completing them in any order; the important thing is to do them all before proceeding to the next phase of the project.

Checklist #1—The Initiating Phase

☐ Capture the objective of the project in 1 complete, succinct sentence

☐ High-level project schedule milestones identified

☐ High-level scope of work identified

☐ High-level project resources (budget and people) identified

☐ 1st draft of the stakeholder management tool developed

☐ Complete the project charter (if needed)

☐ Hold the project kick-off meeting

Checklist #2—Planning

The Planning Phase of the project is where the work really happens when it comes to project mechanics. The team develops the requirements and identifies work that must be completed as part of the project work. This information is then used to develop the risk management plans and the release readiness criteria, and then all of these components are folded into a project schedule. While all of this work is going on the communication plans are developed and stakeholder expectations are actively being managed. These items are arranged in chronological order, but you may end up completing them in any order; the important thing is to do them all before proceeding to the next phase of the project.

Checklist #2—The Planning Phase

☐ Regular team meetings have been scheduled for the expected duration of the project

☐ The communication plan has been completed

☐ Project lifecycle model has been identified

☐ Project requirements are frozen and formal change control is now in effect

☐ Change Control Board has been established

☐ The Release Readiness Checklist has been developed

☐ The risk register has been developed and the top risks have active risk management plans identified

☐ All stakeholders agree to the project timeline milestones

☐ Schedule has been baselined

☐ The committed project schedule has been communicated to the organization

Checklist #3—Execution Phase

The Execution Phase of the project is where all of that planning you did in Chapter 3 gets applied. In this phase, project managers create artifacts in the service of performing the project work; these artifacts include change requests, meeting minutes, and project status updates. Here you also maintain the schedule and risk register by regularly updating them as the work evolves. Checklist 3 is a bit different from the previous two you've used because these items are recurring, meaning that you will do these tasks multiple times throughout this phase. The important thing to keep in mind is that you should be doing all of these tasks; they represent the minimum tasks you need to perform during Execution.

Checklist #3—The Execution Phase

☐ Standing team meetings are effective and held regularly with a stated agenda

☐ Changes to the POR are managed effectively through the project and program-level CCBs

☐ The project schedule is updated regularly, incorporating unplanned work as needed

☐ Project execution metrics have been established, are monitored regularly, and drive corrective actions as needed

☐ Project risks are reviewed regularly, with new risks identified and action plans updated as needed

☐ Project status updates are provided to key stakeholders at a regular cadence

☐ Problems impeding the team's ability to execute the project plan are efficiently escalated

Checklist #4—Releasing the Project Deliverables

The release work in the Execution Phase is a special subset of the work you do to execute the project. Here you leveraged the work done in the Planning Phase to evaluate whether or not the team is ready to release the project deliverable. You pave the way with your major stakeholders to ensure that the release approval is "in the bag" as long as the release activities go well. You enable your team to complete the release activities by establishing and maintaining a low-drama environment. Finally, you successfully navigate the release approval process. The following checklist identifies the major tasks you need to complete as you lead your team to release the project deliverables. The important thing to keep in mind is that you should be doing all of these tasks; they represent the minimum tasks you need to perform during the release process.

Checklist #4—Releasing the Project Deliverables

☐ Ensure all items on the Release Readiness Checklist have been completed

☐ For Release Readiness Checklist items that cannot be completed prior to the release, obtain the necessary waivers and stakeholder approval, prior to the release

☐ Complete the release plan (all work identified and organized into a logical flow, event scheduled, communication plan ready)

☐ Confirm release approval/"Go/No Go" decision criteria with key stakeholders

☐ Complete release activity

☐ Obtain formal release approval

☐ Provide formal notification of release status to key stakeholders

---

Checklist #5—Closing the Project

Here are the major tasks you need to complete as you and your team wrap up the project during the Closing Phase. Many of these items will be done simultaneously. Again, the important thing to keep in mind is that you should be doing all of these tasks; they represent the minimum tasks you need to perform during the release process.

Checklist #5—Closing the Project

- ☐ Facilitate the project retrospective
- ☐ Clean house
- ☐   Appropriately disposition all project material (HW & SW)
- ☐   Post all collateral to their permanent locations
- ☐   Archive important project artifacts
- ☐ Publish project summary
- ☐ Obtain key stakeholder agreement that the project work is complete
- ☐ Hold a celebration for the team (if warranted)
- ☐ Recognize individual team members for their contributions (if warranted)
- ☐ Release resources from the project to be available for other work

Appendix B: Estimation Considerations

During the Planning Phase as part of the work to build the Network Diagram, you and your team need to estimate just how long each task in the WBS will take to perform. This is a quagmire of drama and frustration for the unprepared project manager, so I thought I'd share some ideas and simple techniques to help you chart the quickest route through the swamp that is estimation.

A Few Things to Consider Before You Start

The first thing to understand is that there are a wide range of techniques you could use, so you should pick the estimation technique that best fits your particular project. Some organizations will require you to use a specific estimation method; if that's your situation, then the good news is that training on how to use that technique is likely readily available. However, if you've got to figure out how to do it on your own, your first step is to figure out which one to use. A simple web search will return a huge number of hits on this topic, and that's just overwhelming. The good news is that you can start with the

© Melanie McBride 2016
M. McBride, *Project Management Basics*, DOI 10.1007/978-1-4842-2086-3_13

simple techniques and gradually work up to the more advanced methods—
lookin' at you, Modified Wideband Delphi!—as you gain experience and a
desire to do more in-depth estimation.

HELPFUL TIP WHEN SEARCHING FOR PM BEST PRACTICES

When searching for project management resources on the Web, my recommendation is
to start with any links associated with the Project Management Institute (PMI) as these
are peer-reviewed postings and publications representing what are considered to be the
best practices in project management.

If the first thing to understand is to not get freaked out by all of the literature
about estimation processes and techniques, then the second is to understand
what type of output you need from the estimation. Here you should think
about what order of magnitude your work estimates need to be. For instance,
if I'm planning a wedding, then some of the work only needs to be estimated
in days; however, for the actual ceremony, I may need to estimate tasks in
minutes. It may take 10 days to secure a caterer but only 3 minutes for the
bridesmaids to walk down the aisle. See the difference?

The other consideration here is how members of your team will be tracking
their own work. The tasks in the WBS need to be small enough that each
task owner can wrap their head around how much work remains at any given
point in the execution of a particular task. When I ask the mechanical engineer in our weekly team meeting how long he's got left on the chassis design,
I need him to be able to tell me that he's got 4 more days of work. If that
particular task is estimated at 6 weeks and I'm asking the question in week 2,
then it's very difficult for him to answer that question. The point here is that
your WBS tasks need to be broken down into meaningful work packages that
can be estimated and updated throughout the project execution. The unit of
measure your team will provide their estimates in needs to align with how the
work will be planned and updated.

The last consideration when determining what unit of measure to use for
your project estimates is what will be done with the data, a.k.a. the actual
work applied to the project. In some organizations, this data is collected and
used for billing or budgeting, while in others only the duration of the project
is of importance. Whichever type of organization you work in, it's important
to understand the unit of measure for the work estimates. In the absence of
any specific requirement, a good rule of thumb is to estimate work in days and
limit the minimum estimate to 1 full day and the maximum of 1 to 2 weeks.

Okay, we have one more thing to cover before we move into some specific estimation techniques: the difference between *effort-* and *duration*-driven tasks. Effort-driven tasks are defined by how much, well, *effort* they take to complete. A good example of this is my lawn care service. If I do the yard work myself it takes me 2 to 3 hours to cut the grass, prune the shrubbery, deal with the weeds, sweep the walk, etc. If my lawn care service does it they get the same work done in less than an hour, but they use several guys to do it. The actual amount of work is the same in both cases, but the lawn care service gets it done faster because they deploy more resources. My yard work task is an example of an effort-driven task. A duration-driven task is something like baking a cake. Once you put the cake batter into the oven, it takes a set amount of time to bake. Adding another baker into the mix to eagerly stand beside you and peer through that tiny oven window does not make the cake bake faster. It takes as long as it takes to get to that delicious baked goodness because this is a duration-driven task. See the difference? While you really care about these different types of tasks when you're building the actual schedule, it's helpful to understand the differences when estimating the work as well.

Two Easy Estimation Techniques

Okay, now we get to the good stuff, actual estimation. There are two techniques that are easy to use and will yield respectable results: basic and Project Estimation Review Tool (PERT). When you simply ask your teammates to determine how long it will take to perform each task in the WBS, you are performing basic estimation. On the surface, this basic approach appears to be the easiest and most straightforward but it's actually pretty challenging for your team to do. Each team member must make a subjective assessment of how long it will take to complete the tasks, but how they adjust their estimates for the project environment and any uncertainty associated with a particular task is left open to interpretation.

If the team doing the estimation is experienced and familiar with the type of work, then basic estimation can be a reasonable reflection of how long it will take to complete the work, but you still need to level set the team on how buffers will be incorporated into the finished schedule. For instance, if your team estimates that it will take 6 days to complete the schematic changes, does that include any padding for the time it might take to reroute some of the existing design? Or do you need to add a buffer to your schedule to account for this potential delay? It should be noted that this basic estimation process yields a decent ballpark estimate, but if your organization is tracking actual effort expended on the project, then this basic estimate is not going to be accurate enough. This basic approach can be the fastest, most efficient way to get to work estimates for an experienced team; just be careful with this one.

A better option, especially for less experienced teams, is the PERT method, which factors in the reality of the project environment while still leveraging the experience of the team. Think of PERT as a weighted average where you are balancing the team's best estimate with reality. The PERT formula is

$$PERT\ Estimate = (B + 4M + W) / 6$$

where B is the best-case scenario work estimate, M is the most likely scenario work estimate, and W is the worst-case scenario work estimate. Here you are weighting the most likely scenario by a factor of 4 but balancing it out with the corner cases. Make sense? To perform this estimation, you create a spreadsheet listing all of the WBS tasks and ask the team to estimate the best case, the most likely case, and the worst case. Then, using the simple formula above, you calculate the PERT Estimate. I find that experienced team members prefer to use the PERT methodology and the consideration of the three scenarios makes estimation easier for the less experienced members of the team. PERT is a good "all-round" estimation tool, and it's definitely one you should master. If in doubt, go with a PERT estimation method. Also, since the PERT method does account for the worst-case scenario, you will not need as much explicit buffer in the schedule.

A Couple of Pitfalls

I'd be remiss if I didn't clue you into a couple of big pitfalls when it comes to estimation. First, your best approach is always to have the person doing the actual work estimate it. Often, during scoping or even during the estimation process, an experienced subject matter expert (SME) will figure out the work estimates, and that's a big problem. You see, the SME will inherently estimate how long she thinks it will take *herself* to complete the work with her years of experience and familiarity with the best tools to do the work. If you have a less experienced team member actually performing the work, then it's just naturally going to take longer. Always strive to have the person who will perform the work estimate how long that work will take them to complete.

Further, when the team is discussing the work estimates, it's not uncommon for the experienced SME to disagree with the junior team member's estimates, again because her perception of how much effort the task will take is biased by her own experience. As the PM, you need to be able to referee that discussion so that the junior member feels like she has enough time to complete the task and so that the SME understands her teammate's capabilities.

The second pitfall to be aware of is this: the members of the team will focus on how long they've been given to execute the project versus how long the work actually takes. There's a tendency to shoehorn the work estimates into a timeline that meets the expected project release date, and that's a mistake, especially early in Planning. Yes, you will eventually have to optimize the schedule, but you and your team absolutely need to understand the actual effort required to execute the desired scope of work. I'd bet that you don't have to think too long to come up with a memory of being badgered into agreeing to a work estimate that was too short just because that was what was needed to "fit" the schedule into the expected timeframe. Heck, early in my career, I was the one doing that badgering before I really understood what a bad practice that was. It's what we do when we're so distracted by the urgency of hitting that market window that we lose sight of reality.

The problem with this scenario is that while on the surface that schedule you cobbled together looks like it hits the expected commit, in reality it's just stage makeup, and underneath all that paint is the ugly visage of reality. Sure, you can browbeat me into "agreeing" that it will only take 2 days to develop the marketing collateral, but I know in my heart that it's going to take 2 weeks, so while your schedule hits the commit, there's really a 2-week slip in the schedule baked in. To counter this tendency to force fit the estimates into a desired timeframe, I always position the estimation efforts with my team as our best attempt to figure out what it will really take to execute the work. I also emphasize the fact that we will deal with optimizing and pulling in the schedule later, so the goal is to fully understand the work needed. As I see it, allowing yourself to believe that false estimate is you fooling yourself; the task still takes 2 weeks.

Obviously, I've just brushed the surface of all of the estimation tools and techniques out there. You should absolutely master the PERT method and then look for other tools that will improve the team's estimation accuracy. How do you know when you need to look around for a more accurate method? Simple, just start keeping track of how accurate your estimates are by comparing them to the actual effort or duration it takes to complete the work. Estimation methods can get pretty complicated so just keep in mind how you will be using the output and what order of magnitude you need to get the work done. For instance, if all your organization cares about is whether or not the project will take 2 months or 8 to complete, then you may not need to know that it will take 450 man-hours to complete. On the other hand, if someone's paycheck depends on whether it takes 450 or 475 man-hours to complete, then your estimation tool needs to be more precise. Estimation, like the other mechanics of project management we've been discussing here, can be straightforward to execute; it just takes a little time and energy to master. Calculating the PERT estimates is pretty easy; getting the SME and the junior team member to agree on a work estimate might be a bit more of a challenge. Master a few simple estimation techniques to free yourself up for more "referee" work.

Appendix C: Decision-Making Models

Project teams need to make many decisions of various magnitudes constantly throughout the life of the project so it's a good idea to agree on a decision-making methodology early. This methodology should be identified and agreed upon near the end of the Initiating Phase or at the beginning of the Planning Phase, so let's talk about the four most commonly used methods for making decisions. Here, we will cover the strengths and weaknesses of the models and provide some guidance on when to use each one.

Authoritative Decision Model

First, let's talk about a decision model you are no doubt very familiar with: the Authoritative model. In this decision-making process, there's just one decision-maker, it's usually associated with positional authority, and they hold all the cards. This decision-maker is solely accountable for the consequences of the decision and owns all of the responsibility for the quality of it.

This method will generate the fastest decisions, which is good; however, it drives the least amount of buy-in from the team. This is dictator leadership, and while the team may appreciate the fact that the accountability rests completely with

© Melanie McBride 2016

M. McBride, *Project Management Basics*, DOI 10.1007/978-1-4842-2086-3_14

the decision-maker, it does not promote a collaborative team dynamic. Use this method when immediate and decisive action needs to be taken quickly. In fact, I strongly recommend that you utilize Authoritative decision-making as little as possible to preserve the team dynamic. Of course, there are pitfalls you need be aware of with this one.

First, there's the reality that simply telling a team to do something doesn't necessarily mean that they will do it. It's all too easy to delude yourself into thinking that if you had more positional power you could "make" the team execute your decisions, but that's a fallacy. Because the team buy-in is so low with this decision-making method, you must provide additional motivation for the team to execute the decision when it's made authoritatively. Realize that in many instances that additional motivation is the belief that you as the decision-maker will take the heat if it results in a bad outcome.

The second pitfall, and it's a big one, is that since only one person is making the decision with limited input from the team, this method does not result in the best-quality decision. You see, it's made from one perspective without consideration of the alternatives other team members, with different perspectives and experiences, could contribute to the analysis.

Consensus Decision Model

The Consensus decision-making method, on the other hand, overemphasizes the various perspectives and experiences of the team. Here, everyone needs to agree on the decision and there's no strictly defined decision-maker. Utilizing this method means that you have to broker a compromise across the team but it also means that there's no one accountable for the quality of the decision.

The pitfalls here are pretty obvious. It can take time for the team to come to consensus and since the goal is to coalesce on a solution everyone can live with, the resulting decision may not be the best alternative for the project. This method has a pretty poor reputation for these reasons, but here's the thing: this method results in the strongest support from the team for the decision. If it's critical that everyone agree to the decision outcome, then this is the methodology you need to use.

One place where Consensus decision-making is useful in project management is in the final team assessment of readiness before the release activity starts. As the team gets closer to the actual release date, I ask each team member if they are comfortable proceeding with the release. Every single time I've ignored a teammate's concern or "No Go" response, the team struggled to complete the release or it was a failure. Here's a scenario where you want everyone to be confident that everything is in place for the release activity, and if it's not, then the team needs to scramble to close any gaps before proceeding.

Voting Decision Model

The Voting decision-making methodology is similar to the Consensus method in that everyone has an equal say in the final decision. Yes, this is exactly what you think of when you hear "voting"; everyone gets a chance to cast their vote for the option they feel is the best solution. This method is quick and generates moderate-level buy-in from the team. The catch of course is that the decision is only as good as the voting options, and it doesn't really leverage the collective perspectives and experience of the team. You simply cast your vote for whatever solution makes the most sense to you and the option with the most votes becomes the decision. Like the Consensus method, the accountability for the quality of that decision is diluted and amorphous. Yes, the "team" is accountable for the decision, but hey, I didn't vote to get donuts for lunch ... don't look at me! Joking aside, this is actually a very good method for deciding low-value questions such as "where should we go for lunch?" and "should we do the all-day planning session next Wednesday or next Thursday?"

Many office management software packages allow you to automate the voting, making this an extremely efficient method for making those low-impact decisions. One final thing to keep in mind with the Voting model is that you need to understand whether or not anonymity is important in the process. If you believe there's an expectation of privacy with respect to how each member votes, then you probably need to consider one of the other decision-making methods discussed here.

Consultative Decision Model

The fourth decision-making methodology is the Consultative one. Here, there is a designated decision-maker, but unlike the Authoritative model, the team provides input to the decision. The decision-maker carefully considers all of the input from the team and then makes the decision. This model is a good balance of the Authoritative model and the Consensus model, leveraging strengths from both. The decision is reached relatively quickly with good commitment from the team, and the decision-maker is the single person accountable for the quality and outcome. It should be noted that this one requires that the decision-maker be knowledgeable enough about the decision to ask good questions and seek the right supporting data.

Many organizations use this method for big decisions made by review and approval boards. This is actually my favorite decision-making method and the one I use most frequently to keep the project work moving. The primary pitfall of the Consultative decision-making method is that it's not uncommon for a teammate to disagree with the decision. The business needs and the objectives of the project often trump the pet solution passionate team members advocate for. When this happens, the project manager needs to take pains to explain their rationale and the context that informed the decision. In case a team member is adamant about their position, the project manager may need to negotiate a "disagree and commit" conclusion so that the work can continue once the decision is finalized. As you might expect, the other pitfall with this methodology is that it's all too easy to slide into Consensus decision-making inadvertently.

The main take-away here is that these four methods are tools in your PM toolbox, and you always need to ensure that you are picking the right tool for the job. I mentioned that I use Consultative decision-making a lot in my practice, but what I didn't tell you is that I have to be constantly on guard, asking myself if that's the best tool for the job. Here's an example of what I'm talking about: the planner may ask in the team meeting if she should purchase some additional switches because we seem to be going through them faster than expected due to the current troubleshooting work. If these switches are low cost and the PM has the authority to authorize that level of purchase, then the decision really doesn't need to be made consultatively; instead the Authoritative method is just fine. If however, these switches are specialized components with a hefty price tag, then it makes sense to consult with the rest of the team before making the decision. This ability to sense the best decision-making tool to use and then to seamlessly apply it is an extremely useful skill for any PM.

Appendix D: Additional Resources

Project Management Mechanics Resources

When you do a web search for project management resources, you will find a bewildering array of information sources, which can be completely paralyzing. When searching for project management resources on the Web, my recommendation is to start with any links associated with the Project Management Institute (PMI), as these are peer-reviewed postings and publications representing what are considered to be the best practices in project management.

Project Management Institute (www.pmi.org)

Project Management Body of Knowledge, a.k.a. the "PMBOK" (www.pmi.org/PMBOK-Guide-and-Standards.aspx)

© Melanie McBride 2016
M. McBride, *Project Management Basics*, DOI 10.1007/978-1-4842-2086-3_15

Beyond the Mechanics

Ferrazzi, Keith, and Tahl Raz. *Never Eat Alone: And Other Secrets to Success, One Relationship at a Time.* Expanded and updated. New York: Crown Business, 2014. (www.amazon.com/Never-Eat-Alone-Expanded-Updated-ebook/dp/ B00H6JBFOS?ie=UTF8&keywords=love%20is%20the%20killer%20app&qid =1463158569&ref_=sr_1_2&s=books&sr=1-2)

Gilbert, Daniel. *Stumbling on Happiness.* New York: Knopf, 2006. (www.amazon. com/Stumbling-Happiness-Daniel-Gilbert-ebook/dp/B000GCFW0A/ref =sr_1_1?s=books&ie=UTF8&qid=1463159186&sr=1-1&keywords=stumbli ng+on+happiness+by+daniel+gilbert)

Heath, Chip, and Dan Heath. *Decisive: How to Make Better Choices in Life and Work.* New York: Crown Business, 2013. (www.amazon.com/Decisive-Make-Better-Choices-Life-ebook/dp/B009JU6UPG/ref=sr_1_1?s=books&ie=UTF8 &qid=1463158952&sr=1-1&keywords=decisive)

McBride, Melanie. *Managing Projects in the Real World: The Tips and Tricks No One Tells You About When You Start.* New York: Apress, 2013. (https://www. amazon.com/Managing-Projects-Real-World-Tricks/dp/1430265116/ ref=sr_1_fkmr0_1?ie=UTF8&qid=1467132723&sr=8-1-fkmr0&keywords= Managing+Projects+iIn+tThe+Real+World%3A%3B+The+Tips+and+Trick s+No+One+Tells+You+About+When+You+Start)

Patterson, Kerry, Joseph Grenny, Ron McMillan, and Al Switzler. *Crucial Confrontations: Tools for Resolving Broken Promises, Violated Expectations, and Bad Behavior.* New York: McGraw-Hill, 2004. (www.amazon.com/Crucial-Confrontations-Resolving-Promises-Expectations/dp/0071446524)

Patterson, Kerry, Joseph Grenny, Ron McMillan, and Al Switzler. *Crucial Conversations: Tools for Talking When Stakes Are High.* New York: McGraw-Hill Professional, 2011. (www.amazon.com/Crucial-Conversations-Talking-Stakes-Second-ebook/dp/B005K0AYH4?ie=UTF8&btkr=1&ref_ =dp-kindle-redirect)

Sanders, Tim, and Gene Stone. *Love Is the Killer App: How to Win Business and Influence Friends.* New York: Crown Business, 2002. (www.amazon.com/ Love-Killer-App-Business-Influence-ebook/dp/B000Q9F140?ie= UTF8&keywords=love%20is%20the%20killer%20app&qid=1463158569&ref_= sr_1_1&s=books&sr=1-1)

I

Index

© Melanie McBride 2016
M. McBride, *Project Management Basics*, DOI 10.1007/978-1-4842-2086-3

Get the eBook for only $5!

Why limit yourself?

Now you can take the weightless companion with you wherever you go and access your content on your PC, phone, tablet, or reader.

Since you've purchased this print book, we're happy to offer you the eBook in all 3 formats for just $5.

Convenient and fully searchable, the PDF version enables you to easily find and copy code—or perform examples by quickly toggling between instructions and applications. The MOBI format is ideal for your Kindle, while the ePUB can be utilized on a variety of mobile devices.

To learn more, go to www.apress.com/companion or contact support@apress.com.

CPI Antony Rowe
Chippenham, UK
2017-12-19 16:43